# CROSS WAYS®

**6**
SECTION

## UNITS 51–60

# The Letters and Revelation

Fourth Edition

**Harry Wendt**

**CROSSWAYS
INTERNATIONAL**
Minneapolis, MN

**CROSSWAYS®—SECTION 6**
was developed and written by
Harry Wendt, Minneapolis, MN

Illustrations by
Knarelle Beard, Adelaide, South Australia

**CROSSWAYS®—SECTION 6**
is published and distributed by
**CROSSWAYS INTERNATIONAL**
**7930 Computer Avenue South**
**Minneapolis, MN 55435**
**www.crossways.org**

ISBN 978-1-891245-23-7

Fourth Edition

10   9   8   7   6   5   4   3   2

# A Welcome from Crossways International!

We at Crossways International (CI) are delighted that you are about to undertake a study of the entire sweep of the Old and New Testaments using our materials as your guide. May your journey be fruitful and rewarding, and draw you ever closer to the mind, manner, and meaning of Jesus, the Servant-Messiah.

CI is more than a publisher of Christian education and Bible study materials. We also offer hands-on training in the use of our materials, and we make our materials available to special ministries and missions all around the world. We would be happy to partner with you in *any way* that might help you to share the Good News of God's Kingdom with the people you reach.

The courses of Crossways International have been translated into dozens of languages and are used by all major Christian denominations in numerous countries around the world. We have trained tens of thousands of pastors, teachers, and lay-people to teach the Bible with joy and passion.

## WHAT DISTINGUISHES CROSSWAYS INTERNATIONAL?

### ❶ A Panoramic View of Scripture

CI's courses examine the meaning of the Bible by digging into the *complete story* that runs through it—from *Genesis to Revelation*. We believe you cannot fully grasp the enormity and profundity of Jesus the Messiah's mind and message without understanding what preceded Him and set the stage for His ministry and mission.

### ❷ Visual Learning

All of CI's teaching materials make extensive use of specially designed *color graphics* to help people better understand and remember the written material. These make it easier to share God's Good News.

### ❸ Focus on Jesus, the Servant-King

We are not about biblical study merely for study's sake. The core of every CI course is *Jesus, the King who washed feet*—the Messiah who invites us to follow Him by loving and serving others—as He did. These courses help to *transform hearts and lives*.

### ❹ Tools for Faith Development

CI offers *survey courses of increasing depth* that lead people through the entire story of the Bible—plus *short courses* on specific biblical topics, such as Jesus' parables, Christian stewardship, prayer, the Passion and the Christmas stories.

### ❺ Workshop Training for Teachers & Laity

For those interested in *revitalizing their ministries* using CI's courses, we offer workshops that train attendees, step-by-step, how to do it. We also offer workshops for lay-people who are eager to boost their biblical literacy and steep themselves in Scripture. Call us or visit our website.

### ❻ Mission Around the World—and at Home

CI's dedication to the mission and message of Jesus goes beyond mere publishing and teacher-training. We make our materials available in the U.S. and all around the world in *prisons, hospitals, orphanages, street ministries*—anywhere the need is great but resources are scarce. CI is a *non-profit ministry* that relies on our modest sales and the benevolence of supporters in our efforts to heed the Great Commission to "go and make disciples of all nations."

**Contact Crossways International at 1-800-257-7308 or visit our website at <u>www.crossways.org</u>.**

# The Structure of the *Crossways* Series

*Crossways* is offered in six sections of ten units each. Although each section is available for separate purchase, would-be students of the Bible are encouraged to work through all six sections in sequence to gain an overview of the Bible's "big picture." If they choose not to do that, they should first work through a course that will give them an overview of the biblical story-line, such as Crossways International's *See Through the Scriptures* or *The Divine Drama—The Biblical Narrative*. The six sections of *Crossways* are:

### From Creation to the Transjordan

Creation; the biblical overture; the patriarchal narratives; the Exodus from Egypt; the Sinai covenant and the Pentateuchal law-codes; the wilderness wanderings.

### From the Conquest to the Babylonian Exile

The narratives in Joshua, Judges, 1 and 2 Samuel, 1 and 2 Kings; Worship and Holy War.

### The Preexilic and Exilic Prophets

Introducing the Prophets; Amos; Hosea; Isaiah 1–39; Micah; Jeremiah; Nahum, Habakkuk, Zephaniah; Ezekiel.

### The Postexilic Period and Judaism

The return from Babylon; the history of the intertestamental period; 1 and 2 Chronicles, Ezra, and Nehemiah; the postexilic prophets; Psalms; Wisdom literature; apocalyptic writings and Daniel, the Apocrypha and Pseudepigrapha; messianic expectations.

### The Gospels and Acts

First-century Judaism; Mark; Matthew; Luke; John; Acts.

### The Letters and Revelation

Paul and his letters; the Catholic letters; Revelation

# CROSS WAYS®

## 6 SECTION

### UNITS 51–60

# The Letters and Revelation

# UNIT 51

## John's Letters; 1 and 2 Thessalonians

*Confronting Challenges in the Early Church*

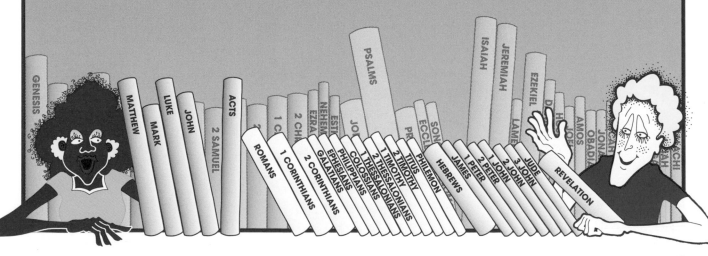

During His ministry in *Galilee* and *Judea*, Jesus had to deal with the beliefs, traditions, and hopes of *Judaism*, and with the political and religious elite who controlled Jerusalem and its Temple system. (See Unit 41.) When the early apostles took Jesus' message to lands *beyond the borders of Palestine*, they witnessed not only to Jewish communities, but also to the non-Jewish world steeped in Greek thought-patterns known as *Gnosticism* (from *gnosis*, the Greek word for "knowledge").

Gnosticism made use of human reason to explain the presence of sin, suffering, and evil in the world. Gnostics taught that although both matter and spirit are eternal things, all *matter is evil* and only *spirit is good*. Because the world is made from matter, it has been evil from the beginning. **ILLUSTRATION 51A** and **ILLUSTRATION 51B** help define Gnosticism.

**1** Although **ILLUSTRATION 51A** uses the ***symbol for God*** (*top left*) used in Crossways illustrations, the Gnostics understood their "god" in ways very different from biblical revelation. The Gnostics said that God is all spirit, and God is good.

**2** ***Planet Earth; symbol for humanity*** (*lower center*): The Gnostics argued that God could not have created the world or the human body because God does not work with matter.

**3** ***Four crowns with astrological symbols:*** However, God created a series of "aeons" or "emanations" at increasing distances from His presence (Gnostics believed that there were many more aeons than the four depicted by the ***crowns***). The farther each was from God, the more ignorance of God each aeon displayed.

**4** ***The fourth crown:*** The most distant aeon was not only ignorant of God, but also downright hostile to God. This aeon created the world and human bodies. "Christian" Gnostics linked this aeon to the God of the Old Testament while maintaining that the true "all spirit" God is the God of the New Testament.

**5** ***Flame symbol on figure and at top left and top right:*** The Gnostics taught that fragments of divine spirit (***flame***) drifted away from God and entered human bodies which, in turn, became their prisons. With the passing of time, these spirits/souls became ignorant of their captive condition and needed to be enlightened (***lamp***, *symbol of wisdom*) with the appropriate wisdom and passwords so that they might escape the body (*matter*) and make their way back to God (*spirit*). Because the Gnostics taught that only the truly intellectual can absorb the necessary knowledge, they made distinctions between those who were capable of knowledge and those who were not—which, in turn, led to intellectual snobbery.

**6** The ***two people*** at *lower left* denote

- **Antinomianism:** Some Gnostics concluded that, because the body was merely matter and would eventually be discarded, they could live as they pleased and indulge the body's every whim and appetite. "Eat, drink, and be merry!"

The ***two people*** at *lower right* denote

- **Legalism:** Others argued that bodily appetites should be suppressed and controlled rigorously lest they interfere with a person's walk in the path of true knowledge and wisdom.

51B

JESUS 'CHRIST' COMES 'CHRIST' JESUS DEPARTS DIES

## Threats Posed by Gnosticism

**1** The Gnostics did not deny that the 'Christ' was divine. They denied that He entered flesh and became human. They distinguished between the human Jesus and the divine 'Christ.'

**2** The Gnostics acknowledged that **JESUS** was indeed a superior person, **ILLUSTRATION 51B**. However, they taught that when Jesus is baptized (**drop of water**), the **'CHRIST' COMES** (**halo**) to take up residence in Jesus' body like a person taking up temporary residence in an apartment. The 'Christ' then empowers Jesus to do miracles and teach (**lamp**, *signifying wisdom*) in order to make known the hitherto unknown God.

**3** When Jesus' passion draws near, the **'CHRIST' DEPARTS** (**rising halo**), and only the man **JESUS DIES**. The Gnostics denied Jesus' resurrection; they had little concern for the human body.

## The New Testament Letters

**1** The New Testament contains 21 writings that follow the Gospels and the Acts of the Apostles. Their names are listed in the following graphic, the third shelf of **ILLUSTRATION 2A**.

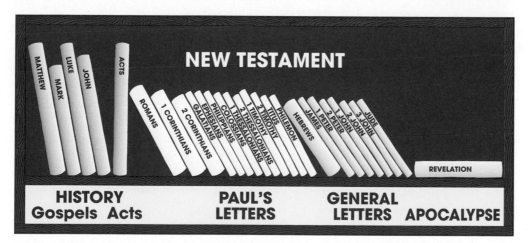

**2** Although 20 of these 21 documents take the form of letters or epistles, some give the impression that they are treatises in the form of a letter—for example, Hebrews and 1 John.

**3** The structure found in these letters reflects the style common to the New Testament world:
  a. They usually begin with a greeting. This greeting identifies the sender and those to whom it is addressed. (In the world of Jesus' day, letters were not placed into envelopes.)
  b. Next comes a prayer, usually in the form of a thanksgiving.

c. The prayer is followed by the body of the letter. In some cases, the contents of this part of the letter are provoked by specific events or circumstances. In it, the writer usually first expounds aspects of Christian teaching and then spells out their implications for discipleship. This pattern reflects the structure of the covenant God made with Israel at Sinai where the *Preamble* and *Historical Prologue* were followed by *Stipulations* (*Indicative—Imperative*).

d. In some of the letters, the writer provides information about projected travel plans, and then concludes with further advice and words of farewell.

**4** Fourteen of the 20 letters are traditionally ascribed to Paul. One of these, the Letter to the Hebrews, does not claim to have been written by Paul. It was accepted into the New Testament only after much debate, and then placed at the end of Paul's writings.

**5** Although the other 13 letters lay claim to having been written by Paul, many scholars believe that some were written by disciples or followers familiar with Paul's teachings (Ephesians, Colossians, 2 Thessalonians, 1 and 2 Timothy, and Titus). They point out that some of Paul's disciples could have written "in Paul's name" in order to gain authority for their own adaptation of Paul's teaching— an accepted practice at that time.

**6** Four of the letters ascribed to Paul are called "The Captivity Letters" because the author refers to being in prison when writing them (Ephesians, Philippians, Colossians, and Philemon).

**7** Three other letters ascribed to Paul (1 and 2 Timothy, Titus) are referred to as "The Pastoral Letters." The reason for this is that they are addressed to individuals rather than to communities, and give advice about caring for the Christian community.

**8** Paul's letters are arranged in two groups: *first*, letters to communities, and *second*, letters to individuals. Within each group they run from the longest to the shortest. They are not arranged in the order in which they were written.

**9** Paul's letters (at least, those that scholars accept as genuinely Pauline) were written earlier than any of the four Gospels.

**10** Paul rarely refers to any of the things that Jesus did or said during His lifetime. Instead, Paul focuses on God's power, working through the life, death, and resurrection of Jesus to save all people— Jews and Greeks alike. For Paul the term "gospel" means the proclamation of faith in God's forgiveness, the proclamation of the "good news" that Jesus the Messiah has come to establish the Messianic Kingdom and to bring salvation to all people.

**11** The final seven New Testament letters are traditionally referred to as "The Catholic Letters." They are defined as catholic (or "universal") because they were addressed to a wide circle of readers and not just to a single community, as were most of Paul's letters.

**12** Three of the Catholic Letters, 1, 2, and 3 John, have close ties to the Gospel according to St. John and are seen as belonging to the Johannine collection of writings.

**13** Although the Catholic Letters are also arranged in approximately descending order of length, the three Johannine letters are kept together, and Jude is placed last.

# John's Letters

**1** In the *First Letter of John*, John insists that God has spoken His true, ultimate Word of eternal life in the revelation of His incarnate Son. Through that Word, God establishes fellowship *between Himself and humanity*, and *among humanity*. Jesus' teaching and mission were God's revelation of Himself because Jesus is God, 1:1–4. John sees in Gnosticism a fourfold attack on Christianity.

    a.   Gnostics denied that, in Jesus, God entered into flesh. Because they denied the incarnation, they undermined the Christian faith, including belief in the resurrection of the body. John answers them, 1:1–4; 2:18–28; 4:1–6,13–15; 5:6–12.

    b.   Gnostics denied the atonement—the central truth that the God-man died to atone for the sins of the world. John answers them in 1:7,9; 2:1,2; 2:12; 3:16; 4:10.

    c.   Gnostics focused on knowledge rather than sin, and felt no need to devote themselves to the service of others. John answers them in 1:8,10; 2:3–11,15–17; 3:4–24; 4:7–12; 4:16–21; 5:1–5.

    d.   Because Gnostics had no use for the material body, they denied that the God-man, Jesus the Messiah, rose from the dead and that the body will one day be resurrected. John answers them in 2:17,25; 3:2; 5:11,12.

In summary, the Gnostics denied the incarnation, the atonement, the reality of sin, the resurrection of the body, and Jesus' call to responsible servanthood. John's message spirals around a series of tests Christians are to take to determine the genuineness of their faith and life.

**2** Apparently the *Second Letter of John* was sent to a specific church, v. 1. John rejoices that some of its members have stood firm against the inroads of a heresy that has been ravaging the church of Asia Minor. Most likely, the false teachers to which this letter refers are the same as those mentioned in the first letter. The letter makes the same emphases about the commandment to love (vv. 5,6) and the reality of the incarnation, v. 7. Similarly, it condemns the false teachings that it attacks as the work of the antichrist (v. 7) and insists that no one can know the Father except through the incarnate Son, v. 9. It contains a severe warning against furthering the activities of those who pervert the Gospel, vv. 10,11. No one is to extend hospitality to them or greet them, v. 10.

**3** Although the First and Second Letters of John deal with a specific heresy, the *Third Letter of John* deals with a problem that arose in connection with missionary work. It was written to a certain Gaius, who had greatly helped itinerant evangelists, vv. 1–6. Those whom he helped reported back to their home church about his kindness, v. 6. However, trouble was being caused by an individual known as Diotrephes in the church of which Gaius was a member. The trouble-maker was refusing to welcome visiting missionaries. He was also making efforts to stop others from welcoming the missionaries, and threatening to put those who did out of the church, vv. 9,10. John thanks Gaius for his efforts on behalf of the missionaries and commends the bearer of the letter to him. He threatens to visit the congregation himself and put an end to Diotrephes' trouble-making.

One of the issues causing confusion in the church at Thessalonica had to do with belief in the resurrection of the body in relation to Jesus' reappearing. The following comments throw light on why that confusion existed.

**1** Throughout most of the Old Testament period, the Israelites did not believe in the resurrection of the body. Although many believed that they would live on beyond death, they thought that they would continue to exist only as a "shade"—as a shadowy reflection of their original form—in Sheol (Greek: *Hades*), the abode of the dead. There would be no continuing communication between God and those in Sheol; God would forget them, Psalm 88.

**2** However, with the passing of the centuries, some of the Israelites—specifically the Hasidim and Pharisees during the last several centuries of the Old Testament period—came to believe in the resurrection of the body and the continuation of life after death. They thought of continuing life as something that would take place during the Messianic Age in the *land of Palestine*. However, those Jews who had ignored the Law or *Torah*, and Gentiles in general, would rise to face judgment and possible destruction and annihilation. The Sadducees, on the other hand, held to traditional beliefs about Sheol and did not believe in the resurrection of the body. On occasion, Paul cleverly diverted attention from himself by referring to his belief in the resurrection of the body—which immediately set the Pharisees and Sadducees at each other's throats, Acts 23:6–10.

**3** **ILLUSTRATION 51E** (*upper section*) depicts the Pharisees' views concerning the "last things" at the time of Jesus and the early church. Death in this *present age* (Hebrew: *ha-olam ha-tzeh*) was viewed as a rather frightening affair (***tombstone and skull***). Questions concerning ***JUDGMENT***, ***RESURRECTION***, and ***ETERNAL LIFE*** would be resolved only in the Messianic Age, the *world to come* (Hebrew: *ha-olam ha-bah*). Many issues in relation to life after death were left unresolved (***question mark***).

**4** **ILLUSTRATION 51E** (*lower section*) shows what Jesus did with these views of the "last things." Jesus assures humanity that He has already dealt with the issues of ***JUDGMENT***, ***RESURRECTION***, and ***ETERNAL LIFE***. In going to the cross, Jesus took humanity's judgment upon Himself. In rising from the dead, He broke death's power and inaugurated a harvest of resurrected bodies—His risen body being the "first fruits" of that harvest, 1 Corinthians 15:23. Jesus assures His followers that, although they will only *enter* eternal life after death, they already *possess* it in this present earthly life. Therefore, they can view death, not as a grim *tombstone*, but as a ***door*** through which they must pass to enter eternal life in all its fullness in the presence of their Lord. Although they know what awaits them *beyond* death, they are to live responsibly *before* death—as compassionate ***sheep*** and not as *indifferent* ***goats*** (see Matthew 25:31–46). While living in this *present (evil) age*, they are to strive to live as citizens of the *age to come*—which has already broken into the present; see 1 Corinthians 2:6,8; 3:18; Galatians 1:4; Ephesians 1:21; 1 Timothy 6:17; Titus 2:12.

**5** When it is remembered that Paul addresses his writings to people living only a few decades after Jesus' ministry, it is little wonder that some confusion existed even among Jewish converts. Even more confusion would have existed in the minds of Gentile converts since they had previously embraced no belief whatsoever in the resurrection of the body.

**6** Early in his ministry, Paul indicated that he expected to be still alive when the *parousia* (Jesus' reappearance) took place, 1 Thessalonians 4:13–18; 1 Corinthians 15:50–57. However, as the years went by, Paul modified his expectations, 2 Timothy 4:6–8. Even so, although Paul modified his view concerning *when* the *parousia* would take place, he did not change his views concerning the *certainty* of the *parousia* and the importance of living the heavenly life in the earthly sphere while waiting for it to take place. Note: The term *parousia* means "presence" or "arrival." It was used in the Greek world to refer to the visit of an important, powerful ruler. Within the New Testament, the term is used to denote the return of Jesus the Messiah—that event in which He who, beyond the resurrection and ascension, *transformed* His presence, will *reappear* at the end of the age, in power and glory, to destroy the antichrist and evil, and to gather the redeemed into His Eternal Home.

## ❶ THE CITY OF THESSALONICA

Thessalonica was an important cosmopolitan harbor city on the Thermaic Gulf in northern Greece. Estimates place its population at 70,000, of whom 20,000 were Jews. It was the capital of the Roman province of Macedonia, the residence of the Roman proconsul, and home for many pagan cults. It was strategically located; its main street was part of the Egnatian Way which linked Rome with Byzantium. This made it a good base for mission work. During the second missionary journey, after Paul and Silas were expelled from Philippi (Acts 16:11–40), they traveled along the Egnatian Way through Amphipolis and Apollonia until they came to Thessalonica (Acts 17:1)—a journey of approximately 100 miles (160 kilometers).

## ❷ PAUL'S MINISTRY IN THESSALONICA

Information about Paul's ministry in Thessalonica is given in Acts 17:1–9. Although one might deduce from Acts that Paul's ministry there lasted only three weeks, Luke's account in Acts is possibly a highly compressed one; Paul's ministry in Thessalonica might have lasted two or three months. (Paul mentions that the Philippians sent him money at least *twice* while he was in Thessalonica, Philippians 4:16.) As usual, Paul began his work in the local synagogue, but was forced to move out of that establishment after only three weeks. He then made the house of Jason his base of operations. The work bore fruit. Some Jews, a large number of devout ("God-fearing") Greeks, and some influential women were converted. Paul's letters suggest that the congregation was a flourishing one, and strong in faith, hope, and love—despite constant persecution at the hands of fellow-citizens and Jews. When the Jews became jealous of Paul's success, they stirred up the mob against him and his helpers, and forced them to leave the city.

During Paul's short stay there, a strong bond of affection was forged between him and the Thessalonian Christians. In the eight short chapters of 1 and 2 Thessalonians, Paul addresses them twenty-one times as "brothers and sisters," a term of Christian endearment.

## ❸ BACKGROUND

### 1 and 2 Thessalonians

After Paul and Silas left Thessalonica, they encountered more opposition at Beroea, Acts 17:10–15. Paul was forced to move on, and several Christians from Beroea accompanied him as far as Athens. Silas and Timothy stayed in Beroea. Upon arriving in Athens, Paul instructed those who had accompanied him to tell Silas and Timothy to come to him as soon as possible. Paul's preaching at Athens did not produce any major results, Acts 17:22–34. The apostle remained anxious about the church at Thessalonica, but for some unknown reason was unable to revisit it, 1 Thessalonians 2:18. After Silas and Timothy came to him at Athens, he sent Timothy to Thessalonica to review the situation there, to build up the faith of the new Christians, and to strengthen their bond with the apostles, 1 Thessalonians 3:1,2. In the meantime, Paul moved on to Corinth. Timothy rejoined him there and reported on the situation in Thessalonica, Acts 18:5. Paul then wrote to the Thessalonians in the name of all three apostles, 1 Thessalonians 1:1. He assured them of his love and affection, encouraged them, and gave them the instruction and admonition that they needed, 1 Thessalonians 3:6–13. He did by letter what he was unable to do face to face.

## ❹ TIMOTHY'S REPORT

Paul begins the letter with a long thanksgiving for the good news Timothy had brought, and for the history of the church there. He then comments on the purity of his motives as the congregation's apostle and pastor. He follows this with a series of admonitions based on Timothy's report.

Apparently, the congregation was being troubled by a few problems. The Thessalonian Christians were living in the Gentile environment of a Greek harbor town where the idea of sexual purity was a complete novelty. They were finding it difficult to practice the chastity that the life of faith requires. Furthermore, the fervent hope they cherished about Jesus' imminent return was degenerating into an excited and irresponsible enthusiasm, with the result that they neglected the duties of daily life. Confusion about events associated with Jesus' return made some despondent about the fate of those who would die before His return. Finally, they were finding it was not always easy to practice mutual love in the circle of the congregation.

## ⑤ CONTENTS

### 1 Thessalonians

a. The Thessalonians have received the apostolic Word enthusiastically; the example they set is known far and wide, 1:2–10. Paul sought to work among them courageously—demonstrating pure, unselfish, and gentle motives, 2:1–8. During his time among them, he supported himself financially and tended to their spiritual welfare with a father's care, 2:9–12. The Thessalonians received Paul's teaching for what it was, namely, the Word of God. That Word worked effectively within them and empowered them to endure persecutions similar to those suffered by the churches in Judea, 2:13–16.

b. Paul longs to see them again, for they are his glory and joy, 2:17. However, Satan is preventing a second visit from taking place, 2:18–20. Because Paul himself could not return to them, he sent Timothy in his place to build them up in the faith and to equip them to stand firm in the midst of persecution, 3:1–5. Timothy has now returned to Paul; his report brought much joy. The Thessalonians are remaining firm in their faith and demonstrating sincere love toward the apostles, 3:6–10. Paul prays that God might make it possible for him to visit them himself. He longs for a personal opportunity to build them up in faith, love, and hope, 3:11–13.

c. In chs. 4 and 5, Paul builds his remarks around Timothy's report. He begins by exhorting the Thessalonians to practice Christian purity in their sexually promiscuous society. They are to treat this admonition very seriously—as one that comes from God Himself, 4:1–8. They are also to demonstrate an ever-increasing measure of love for each other (4:9,10) and to live quiet, peaceful, and industrious lives, 4:11. They are to do this in order to support themselves and win the respect of their pagan neighbors, 4:12.

d. In 4:13–5:11, Paul gives instructions about the final appearing of Jesus. Since Jesus did not reveal when this would take place, it is natural that early Christians desired and expected it in their own lifetime, 4:15–17. Apparently, the Christians at Thessalonica were concerned about those who died before His return. What would that mean for them? Paul writes to assure them that those who are living at the time of the Lord's return will have no advantage over the dead. The dead will rise first and, together with all the living, will go to meet Jesus and be with Him forever, 4:13–18. (Note that, contrary to a popular belief, these words are not describing any kind of a "rapture" of God's people occurring prior to Jesus' final appearing.)

e. Misunderstanding about the proximity of Jesus' final appearing was creating another problem in Thessalonica. Some were so preoccupied with thoughts about it that they were letting their hopes disrupt ordinary activities. Paul assures them that, although the Lord will return, the time of that event is unknown. They are, therefore, to live sober, watchful, productive lives—and be ready at all times, 5:1–11.

f. In the closing section, Paul exhorts his readers to give recognition to their leaders "because

of their work," and to live together peaceably, 5:12,13. They are to admonish, encourage, and serve one another, and to do only good to one another, 5:14,15. Their worship life is to be marked by constant joy, prayer, and thanksgiving, 5:16–18. They should make full, but discerning, use of the gifts of the Spirit, 5:19–22.

g. The conclusion of the letter consists of an intercessory prayer, an appeal for prayer for the apostles, greetings, a request that the letter be read publicly to all the brothers and sisters, and a benediction, 5:23–28.

# 6 BACKGROUND

## 2 Thessalonians

The second letter was written a few months after the first. Apparently, Paul had heard of disturbances within the Christian community there. On the positive side, although persecution was continuing, the faithful were standing firm, 1:4. However, the church was still being troubled by false notions about Jesus' final appearing. Some enthusiasts were declaring that this event had already taken place, and were appealing to a supposed prophetic utterance, teaching, or writing of Paul to support their contention, 2 Thessalonians 2:2. An almost hysterical expectation was causing some to abandon their regular occupations and to fritter life away in an idle, disorderly manner that was disturbing others. Worse yet, it made them dependent for survival on the charity of the church. In his first letter, Paul had warned against idleness and meddling, 4:11,12; 5:14. In his second letter, he uses his apostolic authority to restore order. The letter devotes itself entirely to the twin problems of confusion about the return of Jesus, and the idleness of the enthusiasts.

a. In ch. 1, Paul thanks God for the faith and love the Thessalonians are demonstrating and for their steadfastness in the face of persecution. He assures them that they will participate in the final deliverance, when those who reject the Gospel and oppress the church will be judged by the Lord Jesus Christ. He prays that God will continue to sustain and perfect them, 1:1–12.

b. In ch. 2, Paul instructs the people about Jesus' final appearing. The event has not yet taken place. It must be preceded by the great apostasy and the coming of "the lawless one." The lawless one is presently being restrained. His coming is still in the future. The end will not come until he has been revealed and destroyed, 2:1–12. When the Lord finally returns, God's elect will receive their full salvation; the Thessalonians are numbered among them. God will preserve them until the arrival of that Day, 2:13–17.

c. In ch. 3, Paul exhorts the Thessalonians to pray that the proclamation of the word might bear fruit and that the apostle himself might be preserved, 3:1–5. He exhorts them to discipline those who are disrupting life within the Christian community by leading idle and disorderly lives, 3:6–15.

# 7 TERMS USED

## 2 Thessalonians

a. The term *rebellion* or *apostasy* used in 2 Thessalonians 2 refers to a feature that was common in Jewish teaching concerning the end of the world. It was believed that a widespread apostasy, or falling away from God, would take place before the end. This was to be one of many unnatural portents which would herald the final judgment. The belief is mentioned also in Matthew 24:10ff.

b. The term the *lawless one* (or the *Man of Sin*, the *Son of Perdition*, i.e., one doomed to perish) presents a difficult problem of interpretation. He is spoken of as the emissary of Satan

(2:9), and the one who opposes all forms of religion and claims divine status. He is credited with supernatural gifts (2:9) and with power to attract many followers and lead them to destruction, 2:10. He is even now fully active in the world (2:7) and would be fully revealed if it were not for some restraint that at present holds him in check, 2:6. This restraining power will be exercised until it is removed, 2:7. When this happens, the *parousia* of the *lawless one* will take place, but he and all those he has misled will be destroyed by Jesus at His *parousia*, 2:8,9,12.

c.  Many suggestions have been made about the identity of the *lawless one*, e.g., the Jewish people, Nero, the Papacy, Napoleon, Hitler, or Stalin. The *restraining power* has been equated with the Roman Empire or the preaching of the Gospel. The *restrainer* has been identified with the Emperor Claudius or Paul himself.

Scholars from Augustine (A.D. 354–430) onward agree that only Paul and his readers held the clue to the meaning of these mysterious terms. Possibly, they refer to the cosmic battle between Christ and the Antichrist, God and Mammon, that rages now and will continue to intensify until the final judgment falls on the world—and the power of evil is vanquished once and for all by the power of God.

**51A** When Jesus carried out His ministry in Galilee and Judea, He had to deal with the beliefs, traditions, and hopes of Judaism. As the early apostles carried their message beyond the borders of Galilee and Judea, they found themselves having to deal with Hellenistic culture and Gnostic beliefs. Gnostics focused on the invisible world of spirit, saw matter as evil, and disparaged the material realm. The goal was to free oneself from bondage to the material world and to participate solely in the world of spirit.

**51B** In the Mediterranean world beyond the borders of the Holy Land, some tried to wed Gnosticism to Christianity. Their emphasis on the importance of "knowledge" gave rise to intellectual and spiritual snobbery, and their perverting of the biblical Christian faith resulted in both legalism and antinomianism.

**51C** Of the 22 books that follow the Gospels and the Acts of the Apostles, 20 are letters and, in some cases, theological treatises written in the form of a letter. Even the Book of Revelation might be seen as a letter addressed not merely to seven churches in Asia Minor, but to the church at large that was having to deal with the threats posed by the Roman imperial system.

**51D** Of the three letters ascribed to John, the first two are addressed to believers being troubled or confused by Gnosticism. In his *First Letter*, John states that God has spoken His true and final Word through the teachings and ministry of His incarnate Son, Jesus the Messiah. However, the Gnostics denied that, in Jesus, God entered into flesh. They denied that the God-Man died to atone for the sins of the world. They focused on acquiring knowledge rather than embracing God's forgiveness and His call to devote life to serving others. The Gnostics also denied Jesus' bodily resurrection and the resurrection of all people on the Last Day. In his *Second Letter*, John rejoices that believers are standing firm against Gnosticism. Christians are not to associate in any way with those who pervert the Gospel. In his *Third Letter*, John commends a certain Gaius for showing great kindness to itinerant missionaries, and urges the members of Gaius' congregation to put an end to the trouble-making of a certain Diotrephes.

**51E** Belief in the resurrection of the body does not play a major role in Old Testament writings. However, belief in the resurrection developed increasingly during the centuries immediately preceding Jesus' ministry. In Jesus' day, the Sadducees denied the resurrection of the body and life after death. Although the Pharisees did believe in a bodily resurrection and life after death, they linked hope of entry into heaven/paradise to the keeping of God's Law.

However, those who embraced Jesus the Messiah as forgiving Savior and Lord of time and eternity knew that their relationship with the crucified but risen Jesus made them citizens of God's eternal realm already in this life. Death was not to be feared, but seen as a door leading into God's eternal presence.

**51F** Paul worked in Thessalonica during his second missionary journey. After his stay there was cut short by Jewish opposition to the Gospel, he moved on to Corinth. He was deeply concerned about the spiritual life of the new Christians in Thessalonica and sent Timothy to investigate. *First Thessalonians* was written shortly after Timothy's return. In it, Paul commends the Christians in Thessalonica for their response to the Gospel and perseverance in the faith. He also comments about abuses that Timothy had noted: false expectations about Jesus' final appearing, and withdrawal from the activities of this world in expectation of Jesus' imminent reappearing.

Paul wrote *Second Thessalonians* shortly afterwards. Some in the congregation were saying that Jesus' final appearing had already taken place. Some were gripped by a frenzied excitement and were proving to be a disruptive influence, refraining from work and depending for survival on the handouts of others. Paul states that Jesus' final appearing is not as imminent as many think. The "rebellion" and unmasking of "the lawless one" have to take place first. Christians are to occupy themselves constructively while waiting for the Last Day of history.

# CROSS WAYS®

**6** SECTION

**UNITS 51–60**

# The Letters and Revelation

# UNIT 52
## Galatians

*Paul's Authority, Gospel, and Freedom*

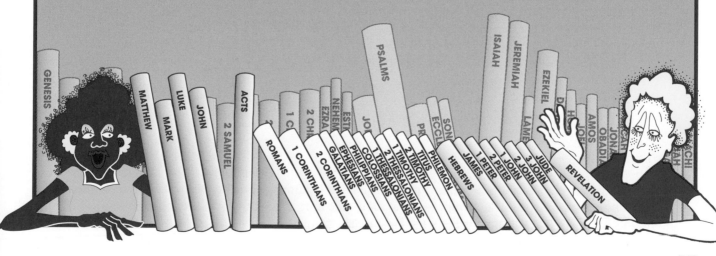

**1** As Paul traveled around the Mediterranean world proclaiming the message entrusted to him, he stressed that Jesus' Messianic ministry was not merely an addendum to Israel's faith. It was the fulfillment of the promises of God! It replaced the *Torah!* Furthermore, the truth God commissioned Paul to proclaim was meant for the whole world, not just for those within Israel's borders. God's Good News declared that, through the Savior of David's line, everyone who believes is set free (declared justified) "from all those sins from which you could not be freed by the Law of Moses," Acts 13:39. Paul threw open the doors of God's spiritual Temple and invited all to enter: Jews, proselytes (converts to Judaism), and Gentiles. He offered all people direct access to God, by grace, through faith in Jesus crucified, risen, and reigning. Paul spelled out what had been implicit in the events of Pentecost and in the evangelization of the Samaritans, the Ethiopian eunuch, Cornelius, and the Gentiles of Antioch.

**2** As a result of this proclamation, a large number of Gentiles entered the church. They did not enter by way of Judaism, or as proselytes, or by submitting to the customs of Moses and being circumcised. They were invited to become full members of the new people of God—just as they were whenever God called them.

**3** All this was bound to raise questions in the minds of Jewish Christians. Many of them could not, or would not, grasp the total newness of the New Covenant—the implications of what John the Baptist meant when he said, "God is able from these stones to raise up children to Abraham," Matthew 3:9. They could not comprehend what Jesus meant when He said, in view of one Gentile's faith, "Many will come from east and west and will eat with Abraham and Isaac and Jacob in the kingdom of heaven," Matthew 8:11.

**4** The Gentile was not to be denied admission into God's family; there was no debate about that. The question was: *On what terms was the Gentile to obtain membership?* Were all Israel's ancient ordinances to be set aside? Were all the tokens of Israel's covenant relationship with God to be discarded? Were all the sacred customs annulled by the new revelation in Jesus? Were the ancient people of God, who claimed Abraham as father, simply to disappear under the increasing stream of Gentile converts coming into God's new community? The tensions these questions created led to the calling of the Apostolic Council (Acts 15; see Unit 50) and the writing of Paul's Letter to the Galatians.

**5** The Apostolic Council answered the question, "Must a Gentile become a proselyte to Judaism in order to be saved?" with a firm, "No!" Another important question remained to be dealt with: "What relationship is to exist between the circumcised, ritually clean Jewish Christian and the uncircumcised, ritually unclean Gentile Christian?" Complex issues were involved. For example, fellowship meals played an important role in the life of the early church, and the Lord's Supper was usually celebrated in connection with them. Could Jews and Gentiles eat together at these meals? Judaizers (those who insisted that faith by itself was not enough and that it was necessary to observe the ritual details of the Mosaic Law in addition to trusting in Jesus as Savior) had a ready answer: "Let the Gentiles be circumcised and become good Jews!" Their attitude made it difficult for people like Paul to carry out what they knew to be the will of God.

**6** The Apostolic Council had asked the Gentiles to abstain from foods and practices that had been a natural part of their pagan past—from foods sacrificed to idols, from blood, from eating animals that had been strangled, and from unchastity, Acts 15:29. It is understandable that unchastity loomed large in the lives of the Gentiles, for it played a considerable part in pagan worship and festivals, and in their everyday life. The Apostolic Council placed a burden of love on the Gentiles when it asked them to

refrain from these practices—so offensive to Jewish sensibilities. However, it also placed a burden of love on the Jews, for it asked just so much of the Gentiles and no more. Because it acted as it did, the Council saved Christianity from becoming a Jewish sect and safeguarded it from the re-imposition of the Mosaic Law (contained in Genesis–Deuteronomy).

**7** The Judaizers did not give up their campaign. They successfully peddled their ideas in regions where Paul and Barnabas worked during the first missionary journey. What did they teach? They did not deny any teachings Paul had brought to the Galatians. They acknowledged and proclaimed Jesus as the Messiah, the Son of God, the risen and exalted Lord, the giver of the Spirit, and the One in whose name is salvation. They did not completely ignore the cross or obliterate the significance of the redemption won on it. They claimed that they had no intention whatsoever of seeking to *destroy* Paul's work. What they wanted to do, they said, was to *complete* it.

**8** The Judaizers taught that, although the coming of Jesus as Messiah was the crowning event of Israel's history, the role of the Old Testament Torah in the life of the New Israel had not come to an end. Circumcision and the Sabbath were permanent ordinances ordained by God as perpetual marks of the eternal covenant God had established with Israel. The coming of Jesus did not free people from the Torah. Indeed, Jesus had confirmed the teaching of the Torah and deepened the obedience it demanded, for salvation through Jesus included most certainly the performance of the works of the Mosaic Law. The Christian tradition, which insisted that salvation was by grace through faith alone, was—according to the Judaizers—a rudimentary and incomplete one. The complete and perfect estate lay in submitting to circumcision and in keeping the law-codes in the Torah—to which circumcision committed a person. Only by adopting this view could one become a true child of Abraham. To dispense with the Torah would lead to a doubtful and dangerous kind of liberty.

**9** Furthermore, the Judaizers insinuated that Paul had not told the Galatians all that they needed to know for their full salvation. No wonder! He was not an apostle of the first rank. He had received his apostolic office from the original twelve apostles in the first place—secondhand, as it were. His failure to insist on the keeping of the ordinances of the Torah was a regrettable demonstration of weakness on his part. Perhaps Paul was so carried away by missionary zeal that he sought to please people and gain converts by toning down the Gospel, Galatians 1:10. The Galatians should therefore submit to the ministry of the Judaizers. They would lead the Galatians to that Christian perfection which Paul's Gospel never could.

**10** The Judaizers, therefore, launched a three-pronged attack on Paul:
    a.  They attacked his apostolate, claiming it was second-rate.
    b.  They attacked his message of God's Good News as inadequate, and said it omitted some of the essential demands of God.
    c.  They attacked his discipleship ethic, declaring that moral dangers would result from proclaiming that salvation is by grace through faith in the absolutely free, forgiving grace of God.

**ILLUSTRATION 52B** contains details similar to those in **ILLUSTRATION 45F**. Comments made about the *upper section* are designed to help explain the message of the *lower section*.

*Upper section*

The **striped triangle** to the left of the name **ABRAHAM** refers to the "biblical overture" to history outlined in Genesis 1–11, in which the themes of Sin-Judgment-Grace play a central role.

**1** God made a one-way *covenant of **DIVINE COMMITMENT** (scroll, arrow pointing to the future)* with **ABRAHAM**, Genesis 12:1–3. In this covenant, God told Abraham to go to the **land of Canaan**, promised Abraham that He would make out of him a **numerous people**, and said that, through Abraham and his descendants, **blessings would flow to the nations**.

**2** At **Mt. Sinai**, God made a *covenant of **HUMAN OBLIGATION*** with Israel. In this covenant, God referred to His *past actions* (**arrow pointing to the past**) for His people as an incentive to encourage them to obey the 613 **commandments** associated with this covenant.

**3** Later, God made a covenant with **DAVID**, promising him that a *dynasty* (**crown**) would descend from him. It was similar in spirit to the one God made with Abraham—a *covenant of **DIVINE COMMITMENT** (arrow pointing to the future)*. The covenants God made with Abraham and David would be endangered and jeopardized *if their descendants worshiped other gods*, and did not, like David, worship one God in one place—Jerusalem, 1 Kings 9:1–9.

**4** The Babylonian **EXILE** proved to be a devastating experience for the people of Judah. Some questioned God's motives in allowing it to happen (**question mark**). As time went by, the people began to understand that, prior to the Babylonian campaigns in 597 and 587 B.C., they had not listened to God's **PROPHETS**. They had served other gods (2 Kings 23:4–14, 24), broken the Sinai covenant, and therefore had deserved the fate that had overtaken them, Isaiah 42:24,25.

Those who returned to Judah from exile in Babylon eventually did away with the prophetic movement, Zechariah 13. They now looked to their *written scriptures* (**scroll**) for "the word of the Lord," and stressed *obedience* to the **law-codes** within those scriptures. They believed that their obedience would prevent a repetition of the Babylonian disaster and hasten the coming of the Messiah. The period of **JUDAISM** (**wavy section of center line**) now begins.

**5** The **vertical line capped by a manger** represents the time of Jesus' coming. To the *right of that line* are symbols of Jesus the Messiah as **Servant-King**, and Jesus' coronation (**cross**), resurrection (**open tomb**), and ascension (**arrow rising from tomb**)—also symbols of the Holy Spirit (**dove**), baptism (**drop of water**), and the Lord's Supper (**bread and cup**).

*Lower section*

**1** God's covenants with Abraham and David found their *final fulfillment* in Jesus the Messiah (a descendant of Abraham and David). Jesus' mission and ministry established a New Covenant that— in a sense—was a "reform movement." While the New Covenant (like the Sinai Covenant) was based entirely on God's grace and goodness, it clarified what true obedience really is, and did away with the notion that "genetic origins" played a role in God's relationship with humanity.

**2** The Torah/Law revealed at Sinai was designed to serve as a *nanny* (more on this term in 52D), to take care of God's people on a temporary basis until Jesus came, Galatians 3:23–29, Romans 10:4. Today, God's people have a new Torah/Law. Jesus' servant life—not the Old Testament commandments—is now the model (Law/Torah) for the godly life. Jesus gives His followers *one commandment*—that they love one another as He has loved them. Although Jesus repeated *some* Old Testament commandments, these serve merely as guidelines for observing His one commandment.

**3** When Paul carried out his apostolic ministry, he usually went first to the Jewish synagogue in the city that he was visiting. Although his hearers were familiar with the Old Testament scriptures, they had to deal with the challenging truth that Jesus was the Messiah, and the New Torah and model for life. Some accepted Paul's message; some were angered by it and sought to kill Paul.

Many believe that, although there are hundreds of religions in the world, they all teach the same thing: "Believe in God and try to be good. If you do that, you will achieve some kind of salvation." In Galatians, as in all his letters, Paul maintains that no person can do anything to earn acceptance by God. God alone is the One who can and does save. **ILLUSTRATION 52C** shows the only two things that people can trust in for salvation. One is a delusion—human works or observances. The other is divine—God's gracious saving action in Jesus the Messiah.

*Upper section*

**1** By virtue of their sin, all people have "fallen overboard" from fellowship with God (***The Good Ship God***). They struggle in ***The Ocean of Sin and Death***. If no means of rescue appears, they will sink to destruction. There are only two possible things for people to cling to.

**2** ***Life preserver*** *(left):* One is something people conjure up by themselves—the *life preserver of good deeds and human effort*. Here people offer up to God what they themselves do. However, this option is not of God and does not create a relationship with God.

**3** ***Life preserver*** *(right):* The other is the rescue plan God has made available in *Jesus the Servant Messiah—crucified, risen, and reigning*. Here, people cling to what God has provided for them.

**4** Every person on the face of the earth clings to one or the other of these two options. And sometimes people attempt to cling to both options, with consistently unreliable results.

**5** Faith in Jesus saves, not because of *what it does*, but because of *what it clings to*—by virtue of its object: Jesus the Servant Messiah, crucified, risen, and reigning.

*Lower section*

**1** People stand under either ***Law*** *(left)* or a ***loving, gracious, forgiving God*** *(right)* for salvation. Paul argues throughout that people are saved by God's grace through faith in Jesus the Messiah. Paul's prepositions are important: *by* grace *through* faith.

**2** Why does the ***person standing under the symbol for God*** not have hands raised in adoration and praise? God does not save the willing (for not one of us by nature is willing), but *makes the unwilling willing*. It is grace from beginning to end. God's children find joy in confessing, "What beggars we are!" At the same time, although we are never saved *by* works, we are always saved *for* works—*for service*.

The challenge Paul faced in dealing with the Judaizers involved more than the notion that people "must keep the Ten Commandments in order to be saved." The issue was also: Is it necessary for Jews (*and others*), who have come to faith in Jesus the Messiah as forgiving Savior and Servant Lord, to keep all the Old Testament Laws in order to be saved?

The Judaizers' attack on Paul was subtle and deadly. Possibly it was under the direction of a single leader, Galatians 5:10. Unfortunately, Judaizers made inroads and claimed numerous victims. They appealed to *converted* Jews by offering them a more comfortable and relaxed relationship with unconverted Jews (in that they could continue to observe Jewish laws and rituals, and see Jesus as merely an additional detail in their faith life). It offered *Gentile converts* a direct linkage to those Jerusalem apostles the Judaizers appealed to as authorities for their cause. No doubt the zeal of these extremists impressed both Jew and Gentile.

Possibly Paul heard about what was happening in Galatia while still at Syrian Antioch after concluding his first missionary journey. If this is so, he was about to go to Jerusalem to thrash out the very question the Judaizers were raising. Because the impending journey made it impossible for him to go to Galatia in person, he wrote a letter to the congregations there.

## PAUL DEFENDS HIS APOSTOLATE
### Galatians 1,2

**1** A fire burns in Paul as he writes this letter. His Gospel is being attacked; God's grace is being denied. That calls for a declaration of war on his opponents. Already in the opening greeting he refers to the three themes he develops in the body of the letter: the divine origin of his apostolate, the role of the cross, and deliverance from the present evil age, 1:1–5.

**2** Although Paul usually begins his letters with words of thanksgiving and prayer, there is no time for this in Galatians. The matter on hand is too serious. Thanksgiving and prayer will keep for another time. What he must do right now is rebuke the Galatians for being so foolish as to let themselves be seduced into believing a different "gospel," 1:6. He is disgusted, angry, and frustrated that such a damnable thing could happen. *There is no other Gospel than that of Jesus the Messiah!* The Galatians must never believe any Gospel other than that which Paul first taught them, even if an angel from heaven or Paul himself were to suggest that they should! A curse on anyone who wants to teach them another Gospel! Paul is not at all concerned about what motives people assign to him. He is no "people-pleaser," as his opponents assert. The very fact that he rebukes the Galatians makes that clear. Paul is a servant of Jesus the Messiah, 1:6–10!

**3** So those Judaizers say that he obtained his apostolic authority from mere humans? They class him as a second-rate apostle? They had better get it straight that he got his authority from Jesus Himself—that very Jesus he once persecuted. God called him to be an apostle and did so out of sheer grace. It is ridiculous to suggest that he got his apostolic authority from mere mortals—from the Jerusalem apostles, for example. *The first contact he had with them took place three years after Jesus first called him.* When he met with some of them on that occasion, all they did was express their joy that the persecutor had become a preacher and was now proclaiming the faith he had earlier tried to destroy, 1:11–24.

**4** Paul had contact with them again, but *fourteen years later!* On that occasion, he outlined to them the Gospel he was proclaiming. They raised no objections. They simply offered him the right hand of fellowship and were glad to hear that God had given him grace to preach Jesus to the Gentiles. The only request they made of Paul and his companions was that they should remember the poor in Jerusalem—and Paul was only too willing to honor that request, 2:1–10.

**5** So Paul's detractors say that he is a second-rate apostle? Well, they should remember that there was once a time when Paul found it necessary to rebuke face to face no less a person than Peter himself.

Peter had been acting inconsistently and deserved the rebuke. When he first arrived in Antioch, he felt no qualms about sharing table with Gentiles in fellowship meals. However, Peter did an about-face when Jewish Christians from Jerusalem arrived on the scene and said that what was going on was wrong. Jews should not share table fellowship with non-Jews! Peter's action called into question the very heart of the Gospel: salvation does not depend on the observance of ceremonial practices, but on God's gift of grace in Jesus the Messiah, 2:11–21.

## PAUL DEFENDS HIS GOSPEL
### Galatians 3,4

**1** Paul throws a question at the Galatians: "Did you receive the Spirit by doing the works of the Law, or by believing what you heard?" (3:2). The answer they must give is obvious. They received salvation by "believing what they heard," 3:5. It is ridiculous to suggest that they obtained salvation through their own efforts, for *God gave it to them*, even as God was responsible for the mighty works that had been done among them. They contributed as little to their salvation as they contributed to those works, 3:1–5.

**2** The only way anyone has ever obtained salvation has been through faith in God's forgiving grace. Consider the case of the first and most important of all Jews: Abraham himself. The Scriptures say that he "believed God and it was reckoned to him as righteousness," 3:6. Those who want to be Abraham's true descendants must adopt his posture before God. The Scriptures nowhere suggest that Abraham trusted in works for salvation. Those who trust in works of the Law as a basis for acceptance by God show that they understand little about the verdict the Law passes on sinful humanity. The bitter truth is that the Law pronounces a curse on any person who does not keep every one of its demands perfectly. There is simply no possibility of anyone being accepted by God on the basis of works. No one can keep the Law. It pronounces a curse on anyone who tries to keep it to earn salvation. The only possible hope humanity has is to place its faith in what Jesus did when He endured the curse the Law brings. Jesus did that when He suffered death on the cross, 3:6–14.

**3** The Galatians need to understand the relationship between God's *promise* and God's *Law*. God's promise, God's original word to humanity, might be thought of as a will. When a person who has made a will dies, his will cannot be added to, or declared null and void. It must stand. Similarly, God's original will (God's promise) was not added to, or declared null and void, when the Law was given at Sinai. Why, then, did God give the Law? The Law was given to serve a short-term purpose in relation to God's original will, God's eternal promise. It was to serve as a custodian, or nanny, over God's people until the promise was finally fulfilled when Jesus came. (*Nanny*: Paul uses the Greek word *paidagogos*, which means "one who watches over and teaches a child.") Jesus' mission means that the Law's time of service is at an end. Now that Jesus has come, all the traditional orders of this world, and all the distinctions the Law made, have lost their significance and no longer apply. In the new order of things, God's heirs are those who have been baptized into a relationship with Jesus the Messiah. In that act of grace, God gives those baptized all they need for admission into His family circle. God invites both Jews and Gentiles to receive what He offers, 3:15–29.

**4** The Galatians should do some thinking about Israel's experiences—experiences that confirm all too clearly that salvation is by grace and nothing else. Although Israel's status under the Law was that of an heir, it was, nevertheless, that of a minor heir. Israel possessed no real liberty and, in a way, was no better off than a slave. If Israel now wants to turn its back on the freedom God wants to lavish on it and go back to life under the Law, it is opting for a life of slavery. The same applies to any Gentiles who

want to act in a similar way. If they entangle themselves in the weak, empty, beggarly elements of the old Mosaic observances, they turn themselves into idolators. If they place their hope of salvation in observing pointless rituals, they cut themselves off from the God who invites them to address Him as "Father" by virtue of what He has done for them through Jesus, 4:1–11.

**5** The Galatians have such short memories! Surely they recall the joy that they experienced when they first became God's children through faith in Jesus. Surely they recall the birthpains Paul went through so that they might be born into God's family! Is it really possible that now they intend to turn their backs on him—on Paul, whom they once loved so dearly? Do they intend to sever their ties with him, and fall under the spell of people whose concern is not Jesus, but their own reputation? If they do that, they will soon find that those who now woo them with glib words plan to lord it over them, 4:12–20.

**6** So those troublemakers promise the Galatians that, if they listen to them, they will learn how to become true sons of Abraham! The Galatians need to have their memories jogged even more! They need to remember that Abraham had two sons, Ishmael and Isaac. If they surrender themselves to faith in the Law as a way of establishing fellowship with God, they will have a sonship akin to that of Ishmael. He was the son of a slave woman and is typical of the covenant at Sinai with all its regulations. This covenant (and the law-codes that were part of it) was no more God's final, saving word than the birth of Ishmael was the fulfillment of the hopes of believing Abraham. Those who submit to this standard as a way of achieving salvation make slaves of themselves. Hagar, Ishmael's mother and a slave woman, has her counterpart in the present Jerusalem (*that of Paul's day*), a city of slavery and doom. But there is another option—God's option. It has to do with the other sonship that is available—the sonship akin to Isaac's. He was born, according to God's promise, of a free woman. God brought about his sonship by a free, creative act. Isaac is typical of the covenant of freedom and corresponds to the *heavenly Jerusalem above*—the free, redeemed people of God. Just as Sarah's son was persecuted by Hagar's son, so also those who rejoice in the freedom of God's Good News are persecuted by the Israel that is enslaved to the Law. Those who now want to be Abraham's true offspring must seek that relationship in the freedom of the Gospel of God's forgiving grace, and not in the slavery of submission to the Law, 4:21–31.

## PAUL DEFENDS THE FREEDOM HIS GOSPEL BESTOWS
### Galatians 5,6

**1** Paul now answers the charge that the proclamation of salvation by grace through faith will result in moral license. Salvation by grace through faith in what Jesus freely gives is incompatible with salvation sought by human effort. To embrace the latter is to reject the former. To make the performance of deeds even a small part of the reason for acceptance by God is to overthrow the Gospel of free grace. To insist that the observation of even a minor regulation, such as circumcision, is necessary for salvation is to deny that salvation is all God's doing. To submit to the slavery such observances impose is to lose the complete and full freedom that faith in Jesus brings, 5:1–12.

**2** Although God's Good News frees people from any need to strive to make themselves acceptable to God through their own works, it does not free them to do as they please. Not at all! The Gospel frees people from the bondage of doing a multitude of things for the wrong reasons. It frees them from the slavery of serving their own self-centered desires and ambitions so that they might serve others in love—God's true will for humanity. The tragedy is that the Judaizers cannot see this. As a result, they are tearing God's family apart, 5:13–15.

**3** True freedom under God means walking by the Spirit—whose one desire is to continue the work of the ever-present but invisible Jesus. It means letting the risen Lord, to whom we belong, direct our lives. That, in turn, means doing battle with the flesh and its inner desires. These inner desires never give up in their attempt to control people completely. To fight them successfully, we need the power of the Spirit. We must, at all times, let the risen Lord determine what we believe and how we walk through life. Our hope of salvation must be based on Jesus. The person who lives in fellowship with Him cannot be touched by the Law's threats or condemnations. Those who walk through life under Law, under flesh, produce one kind of fruit. Those who walk through life joyously under Jesus produce another kind of fruit—they seek to acquire those qualities and virtues that reflect the character and life of Jesus and, therefore, contribute toward the welfare of others, 5:16–24.

4 The Spirit of Jesus leads people in very practical paths, marking the paths of pride, self-assertion, and envy "out-of-bounds" (5:25,26), and pointing only to those paths that lead to the service of others. The Spirit encourages people to demonstrate constantly a meek and gentle concern for those who err—a concern colored by an awareness of their own frailty, 6:1–5. The Spirit also encourages people to practice loving generosity toward teachers in the church, 6:6.

5 The freedom that faith in Jesus brings does not free people from responsibility for their actions. On the contrary, it increases their sense of responsibility. People reap what they sow. They are accountable to God for what they do with life as free people in Jesus. Freedom from obsession to seek one's own righteousness liberates a person to meet the needs of others, especially the needs of those who share the faith, 6:7–10.

6 Paul wrote the concluding section himself, 6:11–18; the rest of the letter was apparently dictated to a scribe. The apostle now summarizes the main points of his letter. He exposes the selfish motives of the Judaizers and contrasts those motives with his own, urges the Galatians to spare him any further agony, and speaks a final word of blessing to the true Israel that walks through life under the Gospel of freedom.

**52A** Paul wrote Galatians after hearing about inroads made by Judaizers into regions where he had worked during his first missionary journey. When witnessing and teaching in many parts of the northern Mediterranean world, Paul stressed that Jesus' ministry was not merely an "additional detail" to Israel's faith. *Jesus' teaching replaced the Torah!* More than that, Jesus' teaching broke down all barriers between Jew and Gentile. People are not declared to be children of God by virtue of their descent from Abraham, nor on the basis of obedience to the commandments given to Moses at Mt. Sinai. God makes people His children on the basis of His forgiving grace.

Not only did many Jewish people reject Jesus as the long-awaited Messiah, but many Jews who professed faith in Jesus as the Messiah and Savior asserted that the requirements and rituals of the old Mosaic Law were still binding—and therefore necessary for salvation. Their emphases destroyed the message of Paul's Gospel. Hence, they attacked Paul's person and apostolate. They dismissed his teachings as inadequate. They insisted that to trust merely in God's forgiving grace for salvation could lead to sexual immorality and a "do-as-you-please" life.

**52B** The Old Testament narrative is a complex one that covers an extensive period of history. After describing the events of creation and humanity's fall into sin, it speaks of God making a covenant with Abraham and then analyzes the history of his descendants. It describes God rescuing His people from bondage in Egypt, and making a covenant with them at Mt. Sinai—a covenant in which God tells the people who He is and what He has done for them; He is their God and they are His people. Only then does He give them commandments. Obedience to the commandments is not to be seen as a way to establish a relationship with God; it is to be seen as a way to reflect the relationship that God has established with His people. Then come the covenant with David, the proclamations of the prophets, the period of exile in Babylon, the return to the Promised Land, and the development of Judaism. In the postexilic period the prophets are denied a hearing. The focus is on analyzing, understanding, and obeying the commandments given at Sinai. Those who obey the commandments will be blessed. Their obedience will hasten the coming of the Messianic Age, and ensure them of a place within it.

However, during the course of His ministry Jesus brings about some radical changes. He clarifies and demonstrates what obedience to His Father really is. He lives the life of a Servant-without-limit. He calls His followers to love one another as He has loved them. In Galatians (and his other writings) Paul points out that the Old Testament commandments have completed their mission: they guided God's people until the coming of Jesus the Messiah. They are now superseded. Jesus' servant life is now the pattern for the life of God's people

**52C** How many "religions" are there in the world? How many things can people finally trust in for salvation? Two—one false, one valid. Those caught up in the world of sin and death look either to *what they offer up to God* (their own works), or to *what God offers down to them*—Jesus' saving work. Only the latter can save and does save. Only the latter is from God.

**52D** In his letter to the Galatians, Paul argues that salvation is something that God has achieved and offers to fallen humanity out of sheer grace. People lay hold of that salvation through faith. Paul did not object if Jews wanted to practice circumcision or other rituals and traditions "for old time's sake." He objected violently to the suggestion that the practice of these and other rituals was *essential* for salvation. Paul's major emphases in Galatians are the following:

- Chs. 1,2: He defends his apostolic authority; the Judaizers were *questioning* it.
- Chs. 3,4: He defends the truth of the Gospel; the Judaizers were *perverting* it.
- Chs. 5,6: He defends the freedom the Gospel bestows; the Judaizers were *sacrificing* it.

CROSS WAYS®

**6**
SECTION

UNITS 51–60

# The Letters and Revelation

# UNIT 53

## 1 Corinthians

*Paul's Wayward Child: Corinth*

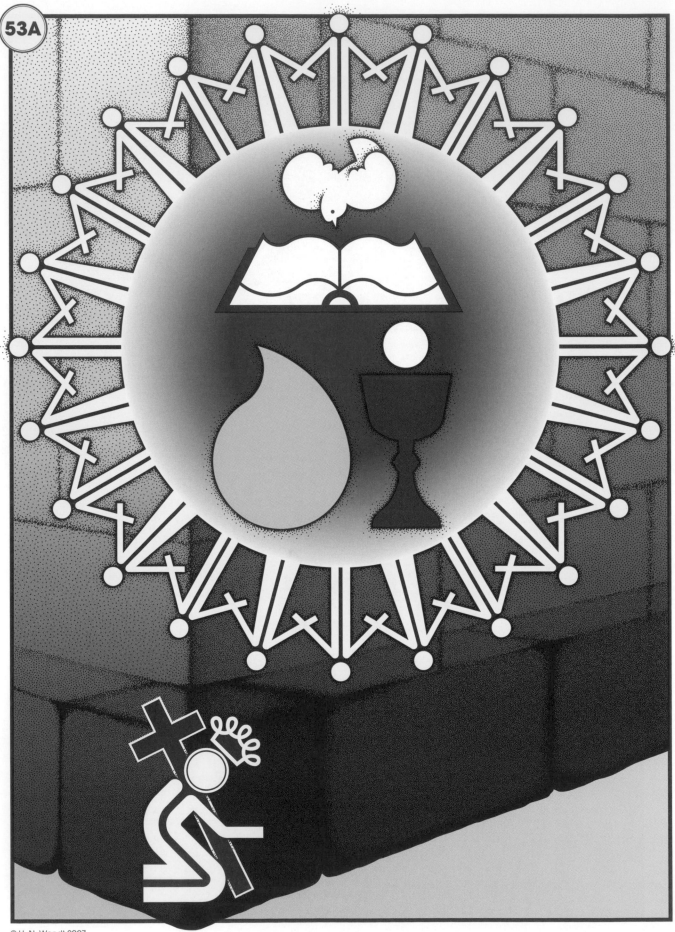

## THE CHURCH AS THE TEMPLE OF GOD

**1** Throughout his letters, Paul stresses a number of key themes. The most foundational of these is that people are saved *by grace, through faith* in Jesus the Messiah crucified and risen, *for service*. Although *justification by grace through faith* is rightly viewed as the hub of the "Christian wheel," many themes are linked to that central truth. **ILLUSTRATION 53B** depicts two of these themes:

- the Christian community as the New Testament Temple;
- unity within the Christian community.

**2** Earlier units provided information about the origin of Solomon's Temple, and the role it and the postexilic Temples played in the history and life of ancient Israel; see Units 15–20. The materials that summarized the Gospel according to Mark (Units 42,43) pointed out that Jesus' teaching ministry culminated in an attack on the corruption and abuses in the Jerusalem Temple, Mark 11:12–21. The materials on the Gospel according to John (Units 48,49) pointed out that Jesus replaced the Temple structure and its rituals with His Person and community, 1:51, 2:13–22.

**3** In a number of his letters, Paul defines the Temple community that Jesus brought into existence, 1 Corinthians 3:16,17; 2 Corinthians 6:16; Ephesians 2:19–22; see also 1 Peter 2:4–6.

    a. Jesus Himself, its ***cornerstone***, defines its *servant shape*.

    b. The apostles and prophets, who were joined to Jesus in grace and proclaimed His saving truth, were the first ***"living stones"*** gathered into that Temple and served as its ***foundation***.

    c. The Spirit (***dove***) empowered the apostles and prophets as they proclaimed and used the *Word* and *sacraments* (***drop of water, bread and cup***). Their proclamation brought others to saving faith, thus making them also living stones in Jesus' Temple (1 Peter 2:4,5) which is, in the final analysis, a ***community of people in fellowship with Jesus and serving each other in love***.

**4** According to Paul, God's plan is not merely to save people for eternal bliss in the life to come. It is also to restore already in this life, in a provisional way, God's original intention for humanity—that all people should devote life to glorifying God by serving each other in community. In Ephesians 1:9,10 (RSV translation) Paul writes:

> *God has made known to us in all wisdom and insight the mystery of His will, according to His purpose which He set forth in Christ, as a plan for the fullness of time,* **to unite all things in Him, things in heaven and things on earth**.

**5** The Christian community is called to be a "provisional display of God's original intention" (Karl Barth). It is the instrument in and through which God is at work to reestablish the original cosmic unity that existed prior to the fall into sin. The Anglican Catechism asks, "What is the mission of the Church?" and answers:

> *The mission of the church is to restore all people to unity with God and each other, in Christ.*

These truths and goals molded Paul's message as he carried out his mission. They also reflect some of what Paul wrote to the church at Corinth.

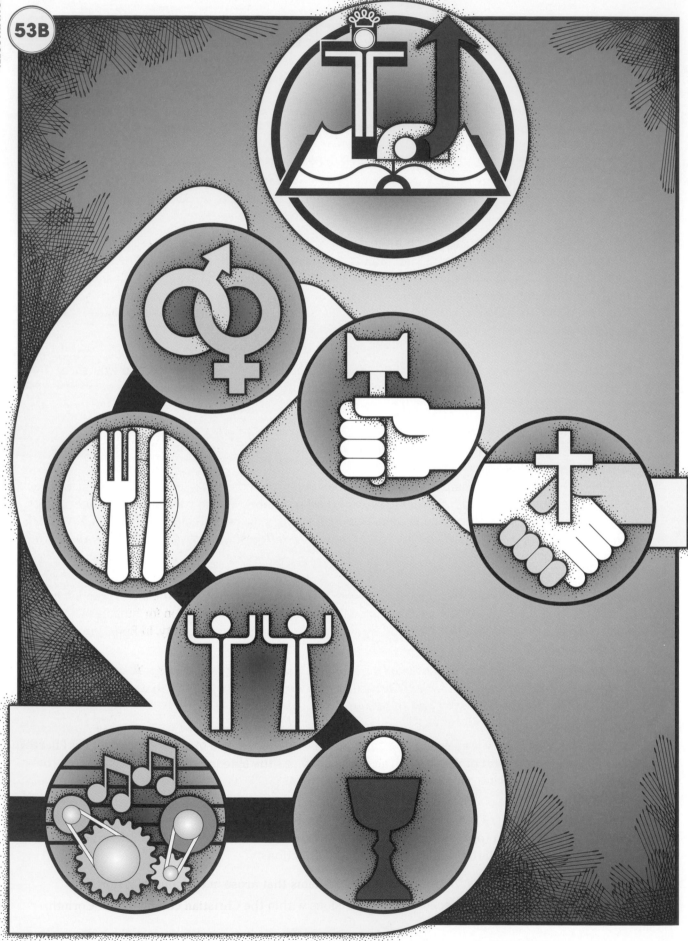

## CORINTH

**1** Greece is almost divided into two parts by the Corinthian and Saronic Gulfs. Between them is an isthmus about 5 miles (8 kilometers) wide on which stands Corinth. Corinth was one of the great commercial cities of the ancient world, bustling with people from all parts of the Roman empire—officials, soldiers, business people, and sailors. It was also an industrial and shipbuilding center, noted for its architecture and interest in the arts. The Isthmian games were held there every two years, and athletes from Greece and other parts of the Roman empire flocked to Corinth to compete. The city's population is said to have consisted of 200,000 citizens and 500,000 slaves.

**2** Every item of Greek north-to-south trade had to pass through Corinth. Because the southern tip of Greece was dangerous for sea travel, east-to-west traffic around Greece sailed up one of its gulfs. If the ship was large, its cargo was unloaded and carried to a ship in the opposite gulf. If the ship was small, it was placed on rollers, dragged across the isthmus, and relaunched. This role as a trade center brought Corinth wealth and prosperity.

**3** The world of Paul's time was notoriously tolerant of sexual license. Corinth had a reputation for debauchery and licentiousness. The term "to Corinthianize" meant "to lead a dissolute life." The term "Corinthian girl" was a euphemism for "prostitute." A thousand sacred prostitutes were attached to the temple of Aphrodite that stood on the Acrocorinthus above the city; it was considered an act of worship to have intercourse with one of them. The historian Aeolian reports that in stage plays, any Corinthian brought on stage was invariably drunk. Such was Corinth!

## THE CHURCH AT CORINTH

In 2 Corinthians 11:22–33, Paul refers to the many things he had to endure in carrying out his apostolic work. In v. 28 he writes, "And, besides other things, I am under daily pressure because of my anxiety for all the churches." One of his spiritual children, the church at Corinth, caused him considerable anxiety. It was perhaps his most brilliant child, but it was also the one that caused him the most worry.

Although Unit 53 analyzes the problems Paul encountered at Corinth and the manner in which he dealt with them, **ILLUSTRATION 53A** summarizes these problems and depicts a key argument he used in countering them.

**1** In Romans 12, 1 Corinthians 12, Ephesians 4 and Colossians 1:18, 2:19, Paul refers to the structure and function of the human body as a metaphor to depict the common life that members of the church are to share in Christ. In the human body, the head directs all actions. Each member and organ is important and has a specific function. Each exists, not to serve itself, but to serve other members so that the body might function in unity and harmony.

In Christ's "body" (the church), **Christ the Head** directs His "members" to live in unity as servants of each other in response to the events of the cross and the empty tomb. Members are to reflect Christ's manner in their dealings with each other and to function as the extension of Christ's body in the life of this world.

In the human body, messages are sent from the brain via a complex system of nerve fibers through the spinal cord. In the church, Christ the Head communicates the message concerning His **servant life**, **cross**, and resurrection (**open tomb**) through the written Word, the Bible. Those not connected to Christ's Word are cut off from Christ's message and directions.

**2** The symbols within Christ's "body" refer to the problems that arose in the church at Corinth:

    a. ***Cross, joined hands:*** cliques and divisions within the Christian community at Corinth, 1 Corinthians 1–4.

b.  *Hand holding gavel:* lawsuits in pagan courts, 6:1–11.

c.  *Marriage symbol:* problems in relation to sex and marriage, 5:1–13; 6:12–20; ch. 7.

d.  *Plate, knife, fork:* problems in relation to fellowship meals and eating meat offered to idols, ch. 8; 10:14–11:1.

e.  *Two figures offering praise:* problems in worship; 11:2–16; 14:26–40.

f.  *Bread and cup:* problems among those wishing to partake of fellowship meals and the Lord's Supper, 11:27–34.

g.  *Symbols of music and machinery:* reminders to Christians then and Christians today that every calling is to be used to render service to others, chs. 12–14.

## PAUL'S CORRESPONDENCE WITH CORINTH

**1**  Paul addressed Corinth's family of God, "To the church of God which is in Corinth, to those who are sanctified in Christ Jesus, called to be saints," 1:2. His letters to the Corinthians make it possible for present-day Christians to learn something about the life of one of the earliest Christian communities. They serve as reminders that those whom Paul addressed as "saints" were such only by God's grace in Christ; as they sought to live pure lives in impure Corinth, their church was plagued by numerous problems.

**2**  Paul established the church in Corinth during his *second* missionary journey, Acts 18:1–17. He worked there for eighteen months and, when he moved on, he left behind a flourishing group of Jewish and Gentile converts.

**3**  Paul wrote 1 Corinthians while working at Ephesus during his *third* missionary journey. Reports reached Paul that the church at Corinth was being ravaged by factions, scandals, doubts, and resentment against Paul himself. In his efforts to correct the situation, Paul wrote four letters, only two of which have survived. A possible reconstruction of the sequence of letters is the following:

a.  A letter preceded our 1 Corinthians; see 1 Corinthians 5:9. Among other things, this earlier letter warned the members of the Corinthian church not to associate with immoral "Christians." Representatives of the congregation wrote back to Paul and asked a number of questions. These had to do with marriage, virginity, the question of eating meat that had been offered to idols, the behavior of women in the worship assemblies, and other problems. Those who delivered the letter to Paul reported that factions within the church were creating tensions, and a scandal involving incest was causing strife among the members.

b.  Paul then wrote 1 Corinthians. In it, he commented on the reports that had been made to him orally (chs. 1–6) and answered the questions put to him, chs. 7–15. This letter was not well received. Relations between Paul and the congregation became strained. The apostle decided to pay the congregation a quick visit to try to put things right. This was a "painful visit"; it accomplished nothing, 2 Corinthians 2:1; 12:14; 13:1,2.

c.  Paul returned to Ephesus and wrote a third letter, one composed "with many tears," 2 Corinthians 2:3,4,9; 10:1,9. Finally, Paul sent Titus on a personal visit to Corinth to try to smooth out the situation. After Titus left Ephesus, the revolt of the silversmiths occurred (Acts 19:23–20:1), an event that forced Paul to leave Ephesus for Macedonia. There he met Titus, who informed him the problem had been resolved and that a reconciliation had taken place.

d.  Paul then wrote a fourth letter, our 2 Corinthians; see Unit 54.

How was Paul to handle his "children" at Corinth? Should he merely attack them for not having severed all links to their former pagan way of life? Although he tells them in no uncertain terms that they have sinned, he tells them much more. He constantly reminds them of God's Good News, God's Gospel. He reminds them of what they have received and become in Jesus the Messiah. He pleads with them to live a life worthy of their high calling as members of the body of Christ. The point and power throughout is Jesus' cross, seen in the light of the resurrection. Paul's opening address sets the tone: "To the church of God that is in Corinth, to those who are sanctified in Christ Jesus, called to be saints," 1 Corinthians 1:2.

 ## FACTIONS
### 1 Corinthians 1–4

a. The Christians at Corinth had enjoyed the benefit of a long ministry by Paul. He was their spiritual father, and their faith had his imprint on it. Apollos had also ministered to them, Acts 18:24–28. Unfortunately, some at Corinth became more attached to their favorite apostle than to the Person the apostle proclaimed. Cliques arose whose members declared: "I belong to Paul!"; "I belong to Apollos!"; "I belong to Cephas (Peter)!"; "I belong to Christ!", 1 Corinthians 1:12.

b. It is easy to understand why this situation developed. Those who came to know Christ became attached to the one (including Paul, hence "I belong to Paul") who brought them to faith in Him as Savior and Messiah. Paul was happy enough to have this bond of love exist between himself and his "children in Christ," as long as the bond remained within proper limits. Christ mattered—not Paul.

c. We learn from Acts that Paul and Apollos worked together harmoniously for a common goal. There is no indication that Apollos sought to enhance his own reputation rather than Christ's glory. However, apparently some within the congregation ("I belong to Apollos") made comparisons between Paul and the personable, energetic, and brilliant Apollos— and found Apollos more to their liking.

d. A third group consisted of those who said, "I belong to Cephas!" Apparently, they claimed for themselves a special connection with Simon Peter and even used the original Aramaic form (*Cephas*) of his official name. Possibly they experienced fellowship with Peter in one of the churches in Judea and later came to Corinth. Possibly they claimed to be representatives of a brand of Christianity more ancient than Paul's. After all, they had been taught by the first of the Apostles—*one who had seen Jesus and lived with Him*. In their view, Paul did not rank with the Twelve. They were members of the "original establishment" in Judea, so to say, and others had made it into the new community only because the "original rules" of Judaism had been relaxed somewhat.

e. Paul mentions a fourth group. Their boast was: "I belong to Christ." He does not describe their position in so many words. However, there is reason to believe that they were from the east and arrived in Corinth bearing letters of recommendation, 2 Corinthians 3:1. Although they were from Judea, and proud of it, they were not Judaizers. Possibly they boasted that they represented the true Judaeo-Christian tradition and felt themselves best-qualified to lead the church.

What was their particular emphasis? It seems that they advocated a liberalism that impressed many people. Although they exalted Christ and awaited His return, they saw in Christ and the gifts of the Spirit a way to personal "knowledge" and "wisdom," 1 Corinthians 3:18–20; 8:1–3,10,11. They said that those who attained this special kind of "knowledge" (Greek: *gnosis*, from whence the word "Gnostic" comes) were made "free." This "knowledge" enabled them to graduate from having to use the Old Testament and

apostolic scriptures. It made all previous standards meaningless and severed all former ties. The result was that they could insist, "All things are lawful for me!" This catch-cry was appealing. Its influence went deep, and it was dangerous.

*Paul responded to the "I belong to Christ" group as follows:* He picked up the slogans of the "new teachers" and gave them a radically new meaning by relating them to the cross. They set forth Christ as the giver of knowledge and freedom. Paul set forth Christ as the Lord of glory who was crucified by the forces of this world. They saw the cross as devoid of power. Paul insisted that they know and trust in nothing but the cross that annihilates all claims to greatness, dispenses with all pretense to wisdom, shuts boasting mouths, and shows the emptiness of cliques that gather around earthly teachers, 1:17; 2:2.

The false teachers boasted of having the Spirit, disregarded the body (a common Gnostic practice), and had inflated religious egos. Paul interpreted the Spirit in relation to the cross on which the incarnate Son of God died in the *flesh*. On Calvary the Creator said a resounding "Yes!" to the worth of the human body formed from dust. That same Spirit empowers people to confess that Jesus is Lord and gives believers gifts to use in love for the service of others within the body, 12:7.

The false teachers boasted of their "wisdom" and created a clique of "the intellectually superior." Paul concerned himself only with the offensive "foolish" wisdom of the cross (1:20,27) that empties humanity of pride and bids it look only to the Lord of glory. The only "knowledge" that matters is not human *knowing*, but *being known* by God, 8:1–3.

The false teachers practiced a freedom that ignored all authority, enthroned the self, and neglected others. Paul pointed to the freedom that made him the lord of all things because he belonged to Christ, and a slave of all people so that he might by all means save some, ch. 9. Christians are set free from the service of sin and self to become servants/slaves of others.

## 2  INCEST
### 1 Corinthians 5:1-13

a.  Paul writes: "I wrote to you in my letter not to associate with immoral persons," 5:9 (within the church is implied). Perhaps it was Chloe's people (1:11) who delivered Paul's first letter to Corinth and told Paul about the influence the proclamation of absolute liberty was having on the life of the church there. The new teachers were saying that Christian "knowledge" set people "free." Apparently, one of their adherents was taking their teaching quite seriously. He was living with his father's wife—probably his stepmother after his father's death. The Corinthian church was not only tolerating this state of affairs, but was arrogant about it, 5:2. Possibly, they argued that those who were spiritually "mature" could tolerate this kind of behavior.

b.  *Response:* The cross rescues people from slavery to sinful fleshly appetites and, from death and judgment, and frees them to live to the glory of God in the service of others. God's people dare not tolerate the presence of impure practices in their midst.

## 3  LAWSUITS
### 1 Corinthians 6:1-11

a.  The new teaching was creating other problems. Christians were not settling their differences within the congregation, but were fighting about them in pagan courts. Possibly the new teachers had little desire to call the errant to repentance and were permitting them to settle their disputes outside the congregation.

b. *Response:* The saints will judge the world! How then can they hand over judgment to the "unsaintly"? They must not hand over the task of dealing with those engaged in disputes with one another to those who belong to the dying world. The church must discipline itself to retain its character as the pure people of God.

## ④ IMMORALITY
### 1 Corinthians 6:12–20

a. The Apostolic Council had requested Gentile Christians to abstain from immorality, Acts 15:29. Apparently, this particular request meant little in Corinth. There the "Christian" man was free to associate with prostitutes; the satisfaction of sexual desire was put on the same level as the satisfaction of hunger.

b. *Response:* The "body of Christ" dare not tolerate impurity within its ranks by permitting a member to join his body to that of a harlot. One does not take that which is joined to Christ and join it to a harlot. Christians do not belong to themselves. God bought them with the blood of Jesus Christ. Their bodies now comprise the Lord's Temple. They are to use God's property in the service of its Maker and Owner!

## ⑤ CELIBACY AND MARRIAGE
### 1 Corinthians 7

a. Fortunately, not all members of the church in Corinth went along with what the new teachers were proclaiming. They raised objections and asked questions. It was becoming increasingly obvious to them that what the new teachers were saying was not only different from what Paul had taught, but contradicted it. Some within the congregation wrote to Paul, posing questions about the new theology of "knowledge" and what the new "moral freedom" was permitting.

b. The first question they raised had to do with marriage. Apparently, the new teachers saw marriage as an impediment to the truly religious life. They wanted "true members" of the congregation to live as celibates. Furthermore, they permitted men and women to sever marriage bonds (especially with pagan spouses) so that they might be "free for the Lord." Perhaps the new teachers permitted those who did not want to marry, but could not remain continent, to associate with harlots, claiming, "All things are lawful for me," 6:12.

c. *Response:* Although the forms of the world will pass away, God's people are to live in the confidence that God has placed them in their stations in life. Therefore, they are to live for God wherever they have been placed. Those who are married may not seek to free themselves from the bond that God has established and sanctified. The false teachers ignore what Jesus taught about the inviolability of the marriage bond and the dangers that can result from the mass imposition of celibacy. Although celibacy has its value, those who take it for themselves run the risk of plunging themselves into serious sin.

## ⑥ MEAT OFFERED TO IDOLS
### 1 Corinthians 8; 10:14–11:1

a. The second issue raised concerned whether a Christian was permitted to eat meat that had been offered to idols. Although the pagans sacrificed animals in their temples, usually only a token part of the animal was burned on the altar; the rest was divided between the worshiper and the priests. The worshiper, on occasion, used his portion for a feast to which he invited his friends; these were usually held in a pagan temple. However, some of the priests' portions (they got more than they could eat) finished up in the market place. This created problems. To refuse to eat meat offered to idols deprived a person of the opportunity for social fellowship and required the removal of meat from the household menu. The false teachers again insisted, "All of us possess knowledge" (8:1) and taught that there was no reason why a "true Christian" should not eat meat previously offered to idols. After all, an idol is "nothing."

b.  *Response:* Jesus alone is Lord. An idol is nothing and has no authority over any child of God. But some are weak in their understanding of this truth. The strong in faith are to practice an understanding love toward them. Furthermore, although an idol itself is indeed nothing, demonic powers are behind the worship of false gods. The church is constantly to keep in mind the example of old Israel, for the new Israel is no more automatically secure than old Israel was. Although Old Israel received many blessings from the Lord's hands, it fell away. The New Israel must take care that the same thing does not happen to it. The members of the congregation must be on their guard, for the attitudes that the false teachers are promoting endanger the faith of those for whom Jesus died, 8:11; but note all of 8:1–11:1.

## 7 WORSHIP LIFE
### 1 Corinthians 11:2–16; 14:33–36

a.  The "new liberty" being proclaimed in Corinth was creating problems also within the worship life of the congregation. Some women were attending worship without the head-covering normal in Greek society. The wearing of a head-covering was a symbol of feminine respectability and an acknowledgment of the place assigned to them by the Creator. Furthermore, some women were assuming a teaching authority that neither the Lord nor the apostles had given them. Apparently, the false teachers were proving contentious about these matters, 11:16.

b.  *Response:* The cross does not do away with the orders God established at creation; it hallows and affirms them. The Christian woman will remember her position in God's order of things, will not lay aside any symbol of her womanliness, and will not aspire after any function in the church beyond that which the Lord has assigned to her, 14:33–36.

## 8 THE LORD'S SUPPER
### 1 Corinthians 11:17–34

a.  The regular fellowship meals in the congregation (known as "love feasts") were becoming events in which the rich gorged themselves while the poor starved. The Lord's Supper, celebrated in connection with these fellowship meals, was becoming *anything but the Lord's Supper.* That which was meant to *unite* the congregation was *dividing* it. Mutual love no longer prevailed. Decency and order were being sacrificed. Some were overindulging with the wine. Edification of the members was being hindered. The clear teaching of the apostles was being disregarded. The example of other churches everywhere was being ignored, 11:17–22.

b.  *Response:* The Lord's Supper is the Lord's gift to the church. Its celebration is to enrich and unify God's people as they share the one loaf and drink from the one cup. Those who turn the Supper into an occasion for carousing, who ignore the real and redeeming presence of the Lord, who observe it with no concern for the needy in the body of Christ, call down divine judgment on themselves, 11:27–34.

## 9  SPIRITUAL GIFTS
### 1 Corinthians 12–14

a.  Some were using the gift of tongues in a way that was anything but edifying. They spoke in tongues even when there was no one present to interpret the message, and they went on and on! They were using the gift to draw attention *to themselves*, rather than to witness *to the Lord*. This practice was fostering individualism, disrupting good order, and giving a confusing witness to those searching for the truth.

b.  *Response:* The risen Lord gives gifts to His people through His Holy Spirit. These gifts are to be used for mutual service and edification. The church is like a human body. The human body is made up of various limbs and organs. Each is different, but none is greater than any other. The human body works in a proper manner only when each part serves the rest of the body. Similarly, "the body of Christ" (the church) functions in a healthy manner only when each member uses life and all gifts in the Christ-like service of other members. Only then can the Church be an effective instrument for Christ. All members have been given gifts, and all these gifts are necessary. They must not be used to pander to the ego and create confusion in worship. God's people must seek to celebrate their faith together so that all are edified, and a clear witness to the Lord is given. The Spirit's most precious gift is the eternal gift of love, ch. 13.

## 10  THE RESURRECTION
### 1 Corinthians 15

a.  Those who claimed to belong to Jesus were denying the resurrection of the body. They were so *"spiritual"* in their outlook that they degraded and disregarded the *material body*. They felt free to sacrifice the very heart of the apostolic proclamation to those Greek prejudices that found the idea of a bodily resurrection particularly offensive.

b.  *Response:* Those who deny the resurrection of the body ignore the central event of all history—the bodily resurrection of Jesus the Messiah from the dead. In denying it, they shut their eyes to all apostolic and Old Testament witness to Jesus. The believer's resurrection is intimately bound to that of Jesus. If Jesus did not rise, the believer will not rise. The converse is also true. If the believer will not rise, then Jesus did not rise. If Jesus did not rise, there is nothing left. The cross is meaningless and has been stripped of its power. It is a lie, and the Christian is without hope. *But Jesus is risen!* The promises that stem from His resurrection are real. Those who ask foolish questions about the mode of the resurrection shut their eyes to the creative power of God. The truth of the resurrection depends on God's clear promises. The person who takes God at His word does not have to waste time with petty, foolish argumentation, but is free to stand steadfast and immovable, abounding in the work of the Lord.

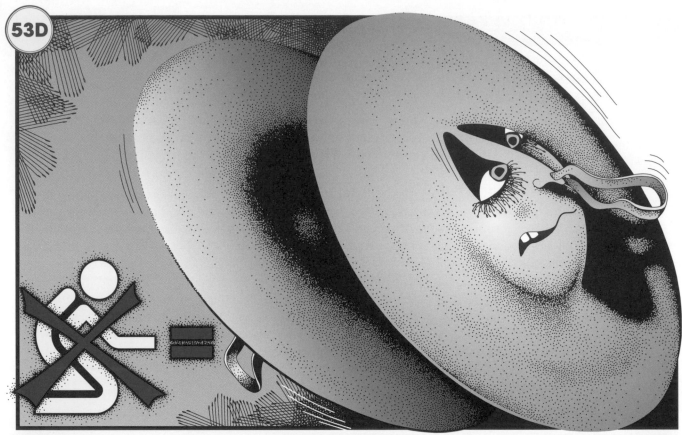

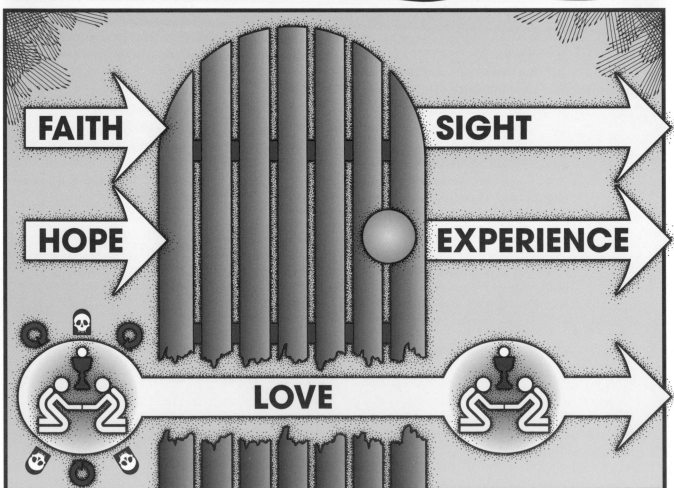

FAITH

SIGHT

HOPE

EXPERIENCE

LOVE

In 1 Corinthians 13:13, Paul writes:

> *And now, faith, hope, and love abide, these three; and the greatest of these is love.*

It might be asked, "Why is love the greatest?"

**ILLUSTRATION 53D**, *upper section*

**1** In 1 Corinthians 13:1–3, Paul points out that a "Christian" devoid of love for humanity (***cancellation symbol on servant figure***) has the spiritual value of a noisy gong or a ***clanging cymbal***. Although faith alone saves, faith is never alone. Faith in Jesus as forgiving Savior and Servant Lord always goes hand in hand with kindness, compassion and servanthood. Although people are never saved *by* works, they are always saved *for* works.

**2** In 1 Corinthians 13:4–7, Paul defines the nature and disposition of love. Behind his message is the thought that Christians are to act toward others as God has acted toward them. Disciples are to reflect their Master.

*Lower section*

**1** This is a graphic depiction of Paul's message in 1 Corinthians 13:8–13, where he stresses that three special spiritual gifts "abide" in this life: faith, hope, and love. Of these three gifts, love is unique in that it is eternal.

   a. ***FAITH*** means "believing in what we cannot see." To illustrate, we believe in a heaven we cannot see. However, when we finally enter heaven, we will not say, "I certainly trust God's promise that I shall eventually see heaven." If we did, God would have reason to respond, "You have arrived! Open your eyes and take in the view!" So, *faith* will give way to ***SIGHT***.

   c. ***HOPE:*** We hope for, and look forward to, the life to come. Again, when we finally enter heaven, we will not say, "I certainly am looking forward to entering heaven one day." If we did, God would have reason to respond, "Hope no longer! You have entered heaven! Enjoy it!" So, *hope* will give way to ***EXPERIENCE***.

   d. ***LOVE:*** If we ask, "What will I do in heaven? How will I use life there?" the answer is: Love, that is, living the servant life will continue into eternity. It is the "greatest" because it will endure throughout this life into and throughout the life to come.

   The illustration depicts ***two servant figures inside a circle***, with ***symbols of the Lord's Supper*** *above and between* them. Around them in this present world are *symbols of sin and death*. An ***arrow labeled LOVE*** points to the right and passes through death (***door with slats***) into eternity where a ***second circle*** (within which are ***symbols of God's heavenly meal*** and ***servanthood***) is depicted once again.

**2** The graphic is not suggesting that love or servanthood in some way earns people the right to break through death and enter heaven. Paul's point is that, in Jesus, the "age to come" has entered into "this present evil age." By grace through faith in Jesus crucified, risen, and reigning, Christians have broken into the "age to come" already in this life. They are therefore to live in this present life as citizens of that eternal kingdom that has already begun. Death is merely a point of transition between "eternal life" in this world and "eternal life" in the world to come. Jesus calls His brothers and sisters to live *now* as they will *then*.

**53A** Throughout his writings, Paul stresses that people are saved by grace, through faith in the crucified and risen Jesus the Messiah, for service to God and others. However, even if faith is to be seen as a personal issue, it is never to be seen as a private affair. God's people are always to see themselves as called to live in caring, sharing community—on a worldwide basis.

One of the images Paul uses to describe the concept of "life in community" has to do with being "living stones" in God's New Temple—in which Jesus "the Servant-cornerstone" demonstrates how His brothers and sisters are to live. Through God's audible, adopting, and edible Word, the Holy Spirit seeks to gather fallen humanity into God's new Temple community, and to inspire them to reflect Jesus in all they think, say, and do.

**53B** Corinth was one of the great cities of the ancient world. It was noted for its architecture and interest in the arts. It was also a commercial, shipbuilding, and industrial center. Its population is said to have consisted of 200,000 Roman citizens and 500,000 slaves. However, the city also had a reputation for tolerating sexual debauchery and licentiousness. The term "Corinthian girl" was a euphemism for "prostitute."

Another image that Paul uses in his writings is that of "the body of Christ"—with Jesus being the Head of that body. Jesus' desire is to instruct and inspire members of His body to abandon the ways of the world and to reflect His Servant mind and manner throughout life in whatever they do.

Paul visited and worked in Corinth during his second missionary journey and established a flourishing group of Jewish and Gentile converts there. While Paul was working at Ephesus during his third missionary journey, reports came to him about irregularities and abuses in the church at Corinth. Representatives of the congregation wrote to Paul, posing questions about marriage, virginity, eating meat offered to idols, the behavior of women in worship assemblies—and other issues.

**53C** The church at Corinth was split into four factions, one of which developed under the influence of false teachers. These false teachers were calling into question virtually everything that Paul had taught about the Christian faith and life. They told their adherents that Jesus came to make available the kind of "knowledge" that would set people "free" to do as they pleased. The result was that the church in Corinth was ravaged by a wide range of problems. The situation was serious. In attempting to solve it, Paul wrote four letters, sent fellow workers to Corinth, and visited the congregation in person. When writing to the congregation, Paul dealt with problems involving;

- factions;
- incest;
- legal disputes;
- sexual immorality;
- marriage and celibacy;
- meat offered to idols;
- worship, and the role of women in the church;
- fellowship meals and the observance of the Lord's Supper;
- the use of the gifts of the Spirit in worship;
- the denial of the resurrection of the body.

Paul dealt with the Corinthians lovingly, but firmly. He attacked the false teachers for questioning his apostolic authority and for the strife they were causing in the congregation. Second Corinthians indicates that the situation was eventually resolved.

**53D** First Corinthians 13:13 contains one of Paul's best known statements. In it, Paul points out that although God has blessed His people with a variety of gifts, three "abide"—faith, hope, and love. Love is the greatest of all gifts. Why? Eventually faith will give way to sight, and hope to experience. However, God's people who are called to practice "love" (Jesus' servant lifestyle) in this world will continue to practice love throughout this life and also the Life to Come.

# CROSS WAYS

**6 SECTION**

**UNITS 51–60**

## The Letters
## and Revelation

## UNIT 54

2 Corinthians

*Opponents and Offerings*

**54A**

1

2

3

4

Thanks to Paul's letters to the Christians in Rome and Corinth, words such as "reconcile" and "reconciliation" have played a central role in Christian terminology down through the centuries; see Romans 5:10,11; 11:15; 2 Corinthians 5:11–6:10, and note in particular 5:16–21. **ILLUSTRATION 54A** depicts the meaning of these words, then shows how Christians today are to understand their relationship to God in Christ. Points 1–4 relate to the four segments of **ILLUSTRATION 54A**.

**1** In the human realm, when two people are on bad terms with each other...

**2** ...a change of disposition must take place *in both parties* if the dispute is to be settled and resolved.

**3** In the divine-human relationship, things are different. Although God is on good terms with humanity, humanity is not reconciled to God. When people are not reconciled to God, they are not reconciled to each other.

**4** Through the cross, God appeals to humanity to be reconciled to Him, and to accept what He offers through the cross. Those reconciled to God are to live in a state of reconciliation with each other also.

**5** **ILLUSTRATION 54A** helps make clear that, in the divine-human relationship, the problem is not within *God* but within *people*. The Bible never offers people advice concerning how to reconcile God to them. God does not need reconciling to people—*people need reconciling to God*. Furthermore, the Bible does not offer advice about how to effect, or bring about, any change in God. God does not need changing—*people need changing!*

**6** People are sometimes asked "Have you found the Lord?" The truth of the matter is that *God* has never been lost and *God* does not need finding. *People* are lost, and *people* need finding.

**7** Although on occasion preachers say to their people, "If you will believe this, then God will forgive you," the truth of the matter is that God has forgiveness available long before people ask for it. God is eager that people become aware of their need of forgiveness and in faith lay hold of what He offers them.

**8** Some medieval theories of the atonement were just that—"theories," and not exactly helpful. It is not correct to suggest that Jesus did something to change God. The visible Jesus revealed the invisible Father. As Paul writes:

> *In Christ God was reconciling the world to Himself, not counting their trespasses against them.*
> (2 Corinthians 5:19)

**9** Although some may argue that the points made in relation to **ILLUSTRATION 54A** involve "hair-splitting," the response must be that the concept of "reconciliation" is central to Paul's proclamation—and God's people need to understand the meaning of the term. When we understand the term, we see that when we sin we do not primarily break God's laws; we break God's heart. Even so, God waits eagerly to receive wayward people back into His presence and family in grace, mercy, and forgiveness.

**1** Paul indicated in his first letter to the Corinthians (16:10) that Timothy would visit them. Most likely, Paul sent Timothy to Corinth to back up the message of his letter. Paul suspected that Timothy's task would be difficult (1 Corinthians 16:10,11) and that his reception would be anything but friendly. Apparently Timothy's stay was short.

**2** Although 2 Corinthians says nothing about what transpired between the writing of 1 and 2 Corinthians, scholars suggest that the following series of events took place. Timothy told Paul about the reception his letter had received and about the way things were going at Corinth. The influence the false teachers were having was apparently greater than Paul had realized. They were threatening the very existence of the congregation. Paul decided to terminate his work at Ephesus and go to Corinth; this particular visit was the "painful visit" Paul refers to in 2 Corinthians 2:1. The visit was painful not only for Paul, but also for the Corinthians. Paul confronted them with some blunt truths, 2 Corinthians 2:2–4; 13:2. Even so, Paul found himself facing some strong opposition.

**3** Those who claimed "to belong to Christ" were retaining their influence over a disturbing percentage of other members. How was Paul to handle these troublemakers? He concluded that he had to sever fellowship with them. Although the issue was not settled when Paul left Corinth, he hoped that the members of the church would realize that they, too, had to break off relations with the false teachers. As Paul took his leave, he assured the members he would return to Corinth in the near future, 2 Corinthians 1:15,16. This promise involved a change of plans from those mentioned in 1 Corinthians 16:5,6.

**4** What followed is uncertain. Paul's hope that the church at Corinth would come to its senses was apparently not realized. There are hints that relations between the apostle and the congregation were strained even further by someone who caused him real pain, 2 Corinthians 2:5. Paul does not spell out what happened. Perhaps one of his loyal supporters was subjected to abuse. Whatever it was, Paul was convinced that the church could not ignore what had happened and still remain "his church." He therefore changed his plans once again. Instead of going directly from Ephesus to Corinth, he went to Macedonia by way of Troas.

**5** Before Paul left Asia, he wrote a letter that he refers to as a "severe letter" (now lost), one written with "many tears," 2 Corinthians 2:4. In it Paul told his opponents that they needed to repent. The person responsible for offending him had to be disciplined. The congregation must come to its senses and submit to its apostle. Paul sent the letter to Corinth with Titus with the understanding being that Titus was to rejoin him at Troas and let him know the outcome.

**6** Paul reached Troas before Titus did, 2 Corinthians 2:12. His agony over the situation moved him to leave Troas for Macedonia, 2 Corinthians 2:13. Eventually, Titus arrived, *with good news!* The church at Corinth had repented and submitted to Paul's authority. Furthermore, it had disciplined the person who had offended Paul and was asking Paul to forgive him. *And the church wanted to see Paul himself to restore good relations with him.*

**7** Unfortunately, there was another side to Titus' report. The person who had offended Paul had been disciplined by the *majority* of the congregation, but not by *all*, 2 Corinthians 2:6. The new teachers still commanded a reasonable following. They called into question everything they could about Paul: his teaching, his travel plans, and his apostolic authority, 2 Corinthians 1:17. It was possibly their influence that held up the project so dear to Paul's heart—the gathering of an offering for the poor in Jerusalem.

**8** The *apparent* reason for writing 2 Corinthians was the unfinished task of gathering the offering for the poor at Jerusalem. However, the *central* purpose of his letter was the re-establishment of a full and proper understanding of Paul's authority as "an apostle of Christ Jesus by the will of God," 2 Corinthians 1:1. Paul wanted to make clear to the Corinthians, once and for all, Who and what gave his ministry its power and glory.

**9** This concern dominates chs. 1–7. This section looks backward and rejoices in the desire of the majority at Corinth to be reconciled. It declares Paul's forgiveness to the offender and assures him of the church's love for him. It appeals for a restoration of the relationship that had prevailed in former times. This issue also dominates the third section of the letter (chs. 10–13), which speaks of Paul's approaching visit to Corinth and deals severely with the apostle's detractors. The same concern is evident in chs. 8 and 9, even though the major purpose of these two chapters is to stimulate interest in the planned offering.

**10** To sum up: In 2 Corinthians Paul fights for his apostolate. In doing this, he fights for Christ, not himself. The apostolate is nothing but the power and presence of Christ among people. Paul's emotions are close to the surface throughout the letter. He reveals himself as an affectionate person, but one deeply hurt by misunderstanding and evildoing. At the same time, he is very happy when he can praise the Corinthians in any way. Although 2 Corinthians is intensely personal, it contains much teaching that is distinctly Pauline in content and spirit.

# Summary of 2 Corinthians

## PAUL'S APOSTOLIC AUTHORITY
### 2 Corinthians 1–7

**1** Paul usually begins his letters with a verse or two of thanksgiving. However, the first seven chapters of 2 Corinthians are virtually all thanksgiving. In them, Paul thanks God for his apostolic ministry. God has called Paul into it and has sustained him in grace. God has comforted him that he might comfort others and increase their faith in the One who raises the dead, 1:1–11.

**2** Paul has to endure many things as he works for the Lord. For example, the false teachers at Corinth twist everything he says. They accuse him of being confused about his travel plans. "He *will* come to Corinth—he *won't* come to Corinth." They do not understand that his real reason for changing plans is to spare them a verbal blast. Despite all that he has to endure, God continues to help him—even as He always has. God is utterly reliable in His dealings with Paul and honors His every promise. And now, thanks be to God, the church at Corinth has repented. The person who caused Paul so much pain has been disciplined. Even so, that person must be shown all the love possible. The congregation has forgiven him—and Paul forgives him. What great things God's grace empowers people to do, 1:12–2:17!

**3** Paul is quite different from those false teachers in Corinth. They need letters of introduction to tell everyone what great people they are. Paul does not need such letters. The church that God has built through him is his *living letter*—one that the Holy Spirit has written, 3:1–3.

**4** Paul is a minister of the Gospel because God has made him one. His ministry is not about condemnation and death. He is a minister of the New Covenant that justifies a person before God and gives eternal life as a gift. It does not concern itself with short-term goals, but with permanent ones. Its glory does not fade with the passing of time. It gives a believer a boldness before God that even Moses did not have. Israel cannot know this joyous boldness unless it returns to the Lord. The Lord works through the Holy Spirit to create more and more glory in relation to bringing people to faith in His saving grace. God makes them truly free in relation to Himself. Paul can preach and teach these things with an open honesty. After all, they are not *Paul's* ideas; they are *God's* ideas, 3:4–4:6.

**5** The apostles do not put glory into their ministry through what *they* are or do; the glory comes from *God*. Those who do God's work may have to put up with many hardships, but these do not detract from the glory of what they do. In fact, when people seem to be weak "nothings," it is more obvious that God is the One who gets things done. Furthermore, it is just when the apostles lay down their lives for the Lord that they most reflect Christ Himself. They lay down life so that Christ might rise up in the lives of their hearers. What does it matter if Christ's witnesses have to put up with trials in this life? God has promised them that He will give them a new body and eternal life. How grand it will be to be with God, to receive those things already possessed in promise! While God's people wait for this, their only desire is to please the One who will one day call them before His judgment throne, 4:7–5:10.

**6** Paul's constant desire is to win people for Christ. It does not matter if people think him sane or mad. He will put sanity and madness to work for Christ. His one goal is to live for Him who died for all, that all might live for Him. Paul's ministry cannot be evaluated according to human standards. Its content and authority are from God. God's grace called forth the New Creation that has broken into this present evil world and has made everything prior to it obsolete and irrelevant. Paul is Christ's ambassador. His task is to tell the world about the sinless One who became "the Sinner for all sinners" to bring humanity into a saving relationship with God. When Paul preaches, he is not asking people to listen to Paul. He is asking them to listen to God speaking through him, 5:11–6:10.

**7** Repentance must never be a flash-in-the-pan affair, but an enduring affair. A true church must live in repentance. If the church at Corinth wants to be the church *of God* at Corinth, it must heed what God says to it through Paul. If it wants to be right with God, it must be right with Paul. "Church at Corinth, don't treat God's grace as though it does not matter. There is still time to put things right between yourselves and God, but that time is *now!*" When God calls people to faith, He commands them to be finished with everything that displeases Him. A person must not run back and forth between the realms of darkness and light. God wants to live in people's hearts as the only Tenant. When the Corinthians have opened their hearts to God, they will open them to Paul. The apostle has a warm spot in his heart for them, 6:11–7:4.

**8** Paul can't keep his joy to himself any longer. He has met with Titus and heard all about what has happened in Corinth. He has not mentioned this until now, because he wanted to thank God for the outcome. Titus has told him that all is now well. The church in Corinth has repented. Paul rejoices and is comforted. Titus shares his joy about the situation, 7:5–16.

## THE OFFERING FOR THE CHURCH AT JERUSALEM
### 2 Corinthians 8,9

**1** Paul is overjoyed about his children in Corinth. He has every confidence in them and encourages them to prove that his feelings about them are right. He warmly encourages them to give generously to the offering being taken up for the poor in Jerusalem. The Macedonians have set a good example for the Corinthians to follow. Despite their poverty, they gave generously. The reason they did this was that they first gave *themselves* to God and His apostle. When people do that, their problems are over. They understand that money is merely an extension of self, 8:1–7.

**2** Paul will not resort to commands and orders about the offering. He simply reminds the Corinthians of what they already know: Christ's mercy. Although Christ was rich, He became poor to make the poor rich. The proposed offering is not new to the Corinthians; they began planning for it during the previous year, 8:8–15.

**3** Paul is sending Titus and two others to help with the arrangements. The apostle is sure that his confidence in the church at Corinth is not misplaced. He knows that their response will prove their love, and that they will not drag their feet in seeing the project through. It would be a pity if the delegation taking the money to Jerusalem were to arrive at Corinth and find arrangements incomplete, 8:16–9:5.

**4** There is more to the offering than the mechanics of it. Those who give generously reap a bountiful harvest, and those who receive the gift will be given cause to praise God. Paul began this section with a reference to the grace of God. He concludes it the same way: "Thanks be to God for His indescribable gift!" 9:6–15.

## PAUL CONFRONTS HIS OPPONENTS AND THEIR SUPPORTERS
### 2 Corinthians 10–13

Paul's theme throughout has been the reconciling grace of God. He has stressed how that reconciling grace bound him and the church at Corinth together in the past. He has urged its members to give generously. However, a certain problem remains—the continuing presence in Corinth of the false teachers. They remain

as stubborn as ever. There is no hope of reconciliation with them. No wonder that they oppose Paul. They are full of ideas about their own greatness, while Paul is not one bit interested in human greatness—including his own. Paul wants absolutely nothing to do with cliques. The fact that there are some at Corinth who name their clique after him does not impress him at all. So far as his opponents are concerned, they tear down what he affirms. Paul must show them up for what they really are, and must urge the congregation to have nothing to do with them.

**1** The first thing Paul does is to list the accusations they level at him. They say that he makes a lot of noise when he is a safe distance away, but as soon as he arrives on the scene he becomes meek and mild. He writes violent letters, but is unattractive in appearance and boring to listen to. He can't hold a candle to them! Paul answers by begging them not to push him too far. He does not want to be forced into a position where he has no choice other than to make full use of his apostolic authority. He prefers to use his authority, as he always has, to build up the church and to wait for repentance. He prefers to use stern measures only as a last resort, 10:1–11.

**2** Paul's opponents spend a lot of time commending *themselves*. However, the *Lord* has commended Paul—proof of which is that the Lord used him to establish the church at Corinth. Paul makes it a practice never to trespass where another apostle is working—which is more than his opponents can say! Paul's boast is in the Lord alone. His hope is that the Lord will permit him to bear witness in even more regions. When this happens, his apostolic authority will be vindicated still more—and the Corinthians' *faith* will grow while Paul's *parish* grows, 10:12–18.

**3** The apostle then indulges in a little tongue-in-cheek boasting (his opponents are rather good at doing that!). Paul can outdo them—but with boasting of a different kind altogether. His desire is to protect his church from the inroads of these peddlers of "another Jesus," 11:4. They may be better orators than he is, but his knowledge surpasses theirs, 11:5,6. He will even boast about the fact that he works without pay, even though his opponents point to that to justify their contention that he is a second-rate apostle, 11:7–15.

**4** Furthermore, Paul can far surpass them when it comes to making lists of difficulties encountered in the course of duty, 11:16–33. Although some might argue that these things show how weak Paul is, the real point is that they show how great God must be to get so much done through one so weak. Paul can also outdo his opponents regarding visions and revelations from the Lord. But even as he does this, he is conscious of the thorn-in-the-flesh that the Lord will not remove from him. However, that thorn-in-the-flesh does not matter; it serves to highlight God's power to get things done through Paul—despite his weakness, 12:1–10. (There has been much speculation over the centuries as to the nature of Paul's "thorn-in-the-flesh." It remains a mystery.)

**5** Paul's so-called weaknesses do not make him inferior to these "super-apostles" (12:11) who oppose him. He can point to all the things the Lord accomplished through him at Corinth: signs, wonders, and mighty works. They indicate that the Corinthian church was not served by some second-rate apostle who did not consider his services worthy of pay. (He would not take money from them directly or through his assistants!) Those who twist the truth about his motives for adopting this policy toward salary are guilty of insidious lies. Paul's attitude toward taking money grew out of fatherly concern for people. He has no intention of changing his practice at this point in life, 12:11–18.

**6** Paul's only reason for "boasting" is to strengthen the bond between the Corinthians and God. He is not one bit interested in justifying his actions. All he asks is that they repent before his impending arrival, so that they might be spared the grief of another painful visit, 12:19–21.

**7** In 13:1–10, Paul speaks of the approaching visit. He will deal severely with those who do not repent, and exercise his apostolic authority to the fullest with them. He does not want to act that way. He urges his readers to "do what is right" even if he "may seem to have failed" (13:7), so that there will be no need for him to demonstrate the authority he has been given by Christ who speaks through him.

**8** The letter closes with an admonition, greetings, and a benediction (13:11–13), e.g., "Put things in order, listen to my appeal, agree with one another, live in peace," 13:11.

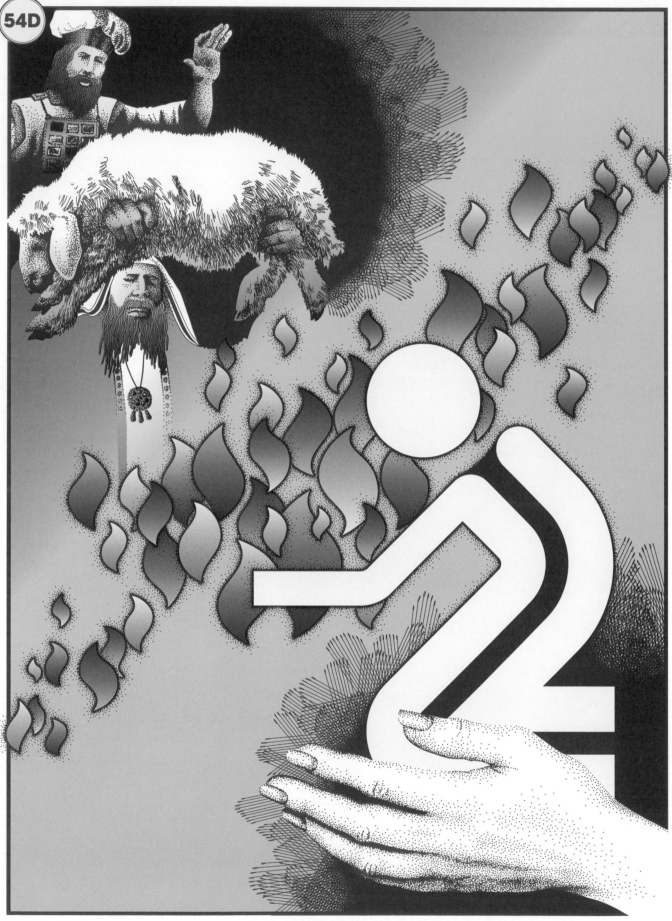

**ILLUSTRATION 54D** highlights a point that is basic to Paul's appeals for response to God's saving action in Christ, including what Paul has to say in 2 Corinthians 8 and 9.

**1** In encouraging the Christians at Corinth to give generously to the offering being taken up for the Christian community in Jerusalem, Paul makes reference to the example of the Macedonian Christians in relation to the project. He points out that they gave with overflowing generosity to the offering because they had first determined *to give themselves to the Lord*, 8:5.

**2** In Romans 12:1, Paul writes, "I appeal to you therefore, brothers and sisters, by the mercies of God, to present your bodies as a living sacrifice, holy and acceptable to God, which is your spiritual worship." Paul's point is that, with the coming of Jesus, the Old Testament sacrificial system has been fulfilled and superseded. However, the concept of sacrifice as such has not been abolished, but transformed. God's people are no longer required to offer a variety of animals or the produce of nature in sacrifice to God; *they are to offer Him their very bodies*. These bodies are to be offered, not to the flames, but in loving service to others (***servant figure***)—and so to God.

**3** Again and again, Paul spells out who God is and what God has done for the salvation of humanity through Christ (*God's indicatives*); he then appeals for the appropriate response from his readers (*God's imperatives*). In 1 Corinthians 15:1–57, for example, Paul spells out what the resurrection of Jesus means for God's people (*indicatives*) and then adds a final *imperative* in the closing verse of the chapter:

> *Therefore, my beloved, be steadfast, immovable, always excelling in the work of the Lord, because you know that in the Lord your labor is not in vain.*

The implications of Paul's message for the life of God's people today are considerable.

Has 2 Corinthians come down to us in its original form? Have parts of it been lost? Have sections been added to it—either by someone else or from some other work of Paul? The transition from 6:13 to 6:14 is so abrupt, and the change of mood at the beginning of ch. 10 so obvious, that some suggest that 2 Corinthians is not a single letter, but a composite of three letters, all admittedly from the pen of Paul. Some scholars suggest that 6:14–7:1 is a fragment of the letter referred to in 1 Corinthians 5:9, and that 2 Corinthians 10–13 is part of the "severe letter" referred to in 2 Corinthians 2:3ff; 7:8. These suggestions might be answered as follows:

**1** All the ancient manuscripts contain 2 Corinthians as we have it today.

**2** It makes more sense to assume that Paul wrote the letter as it stands. An editor trying to weld parts into a unity would smooth over harsh transitions. Paul, writing in the heat and passion of the moment, would not be too concerned about such things.

**3** The question might be asked: "Why were just three fragments of other letters preserved, and not the complete letters?"

**4** Chs. 10–13 do not fit the situation presupposed for the so-called "intermediate letter." They contain no reference to the person who injured Paul or to the sending of Titus.

**5** The sequence of 2 Corinthians makes good sense as it stands.
   a. The first section (1–7) deals with the past.
   b. The second section (8,9) deals with the present.
   c. The third (10–13) deals with the future; the issue of the opposition and disobedience of some at Corinth still had to be dealt with.

**54A** After writing his first letter to the Corinthians, Paul's relationship with the church at Corinth remained strained. In seeking to heal the breach between God, himself, and the Corinthians, Paul exhorted them to be reconciled to God—and also to himself. Paul uses the concept of "reconciliation" in both 2 Corinthians and Romans. He never uses the term to exhort his readers to work at reconciling God to themselves; God needs no reconciling to anyone! However, humanity needs reconciling to God—and beyond that, to each other. God is for us! When we understand that truth, we are to embrace it in faith and joy, and reflect it throughout life.

**54B** Paul wrote his first letter to Corinth while working in Ephesus. His anxiety about the situation in Corinth moved him to leave Ephesus. Scholars believe that, prior to leaving Ephesus, Paul wrote several letters to the Corinthians—including one referred to as the "severe letter." Titus, who delivered the letter, eventually rejoined Paul in Macedonia and reported that the letter had achieved the desired effect. Paul then wrote 2 Corinthians.

**54C** The first seven chapters of 2 Corinthians are virtually all thanksgiving. Throughout, Paul thanks God for the ministry to which he has been called. God has sustained and comforted him so that he might persist in his ministry—no matter what! Although some in Corinth questioned Paul's apostolic authority, Paul defends it. And—thank God!—the church at Corinth has repented. The person who caused Paul so much pain has been disciplined. Even so, that person must be shown all the love possible. The only hope for the life to come, and for meaningful life in this present world, is to embrace the glorious truths that God has revealed in His Word and through the forgiving, servant ministry of Jesus the Messiah. Paul has no desire that people should applaud and praise him. To God alone be all glory! However, if the Corinthians want to be right with God they must also be right with Paul. Repentance is not a short-term affair; it is a life-long affair.

In chs. 8,9, although Paul continues to express his joy with regard to what has taken place in Corinth, he now exhorts the Christians there to join other Macedonians in gathering an offering for the poor in Jerusalem. Despite their poverty, the Macedonians gave generously. In determining how they might respond to Paul's invitation concerning the offering, the Corinthians are to remember that although Jesus was rich, He became poor to make the poor rich. Paul will send Titus and two other workers to Corinth to help with the arrangements.

In chs. 10–13, Paul confronts his opponents and their supporters—whose focus is their own desires and ambitions. Paul wants nothing to do with members of cliques who seek greatness for themselves. So, Paul lists the accusations that his opponents level against him. They make a lot of noise when Paul is far away, but become quiet when he visits with them. Paul has no desire to intrude into regions where others are working faithfully. His constant hope is that God will expand the scope of his ministry. He is not one bit interested in payment for service rendered. The all-powerful God can and does achieve amazing things through a weak Paul!

**54D** When encouraging the church in Corinth to participate in gathering an offering for the poor in Jerusalem, Paul reminds them that they are first to give *themselves* to the Lord. To do so is to honor the radical change that Jesus brought about in that He never commanded His followers to participate in animal sacrifice within the precincts of the Jerusalem Temple. Rather, He exhorted them to offer life in the service of others every moment of every day. After all, if Jesus gave His all for His people, they are to give their all to glorify God by serving others. That is God's definition of His desired sacrificial system.

**54E** Much debate continues to take place concerning how best to understand Paul's correspondence with the church at Corinth. Some suggest that 2 Corinthians is a compilation of three letters—all from the pen of Paul. Others suggest that fragments of other Pauline writings have been incorporated into the letter. However, the sequence of materials within 2 Corinthians makes good sense as it stands. All ancient manuscripts contain 2 Corinthians as we have it today.

# CROSS WAYS

## 6 SECTION

## UNITS 51–60

# The Letters and Revelation

# UNIT 55
## Romans

*The New and True Israel*

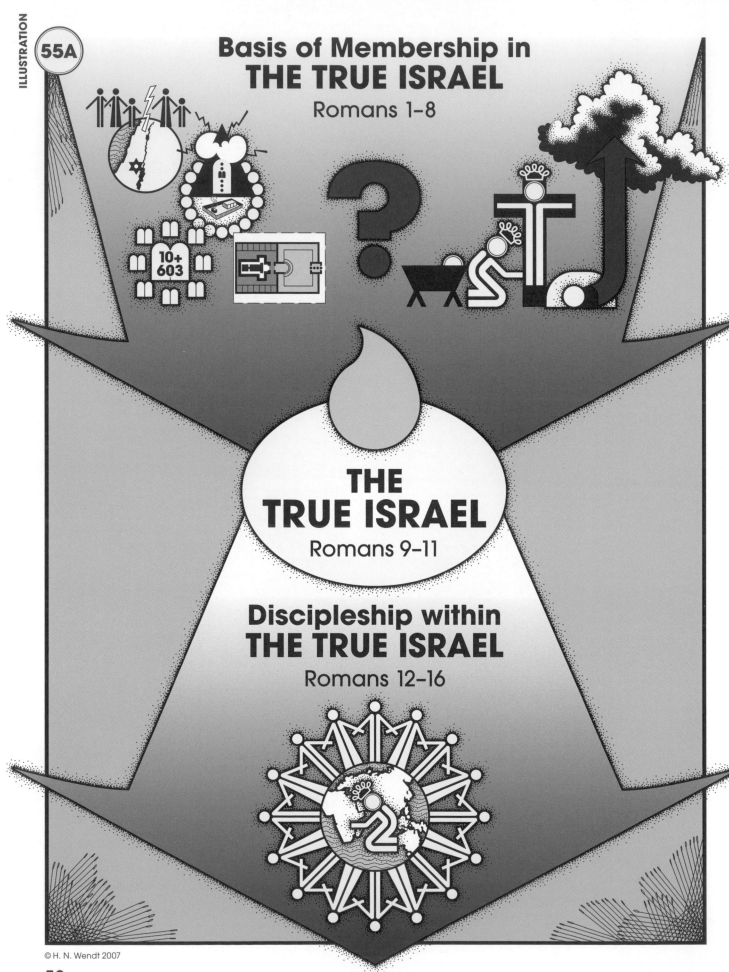

# Basis of Membership in
# THE TRUE ISRAEL
## Romans 1-8

10+
603

?

# THE
# TRUE ISRAEL
## Romans 9-11

# Discipleship within
# THE TRUE ISRAEL
## Romans 12-16

© H. N. Wendt 2007

## OCCASION AND PURPOSE

**1** Most likely, Paul wrote to the church at Rome from Corinth about A.D. 56–57 during his third missionary journey. Although he had never been to Rome, he had heard about the Christian community there and knew some of its members, Romans 16.

**2** Paul wrote at a time when he was making important decisions about his future missionary endeavors. A cause that had long been close to his heart was the plan to gather up a monetary offering from the younger churches around the Mediterranean to give to the mother church in Palestine. Finally the dream became a reality, and Paul set out to take the offering back to Jerusalem. Representatives from the contributing churches accompanied him, Acts 20:4.

**3** Paul planned to work in the western Mediterranean region after delivering the offering, Romans 15:22–29. Because Paul had not previously worked in that part of the world, he needed a base of operations for the project—the natural choice for which was Rome. The idea of going to Rome and working there had long fascinated him. He wrote to introduce himself to the members of the Christian community there to inform them of his intentions, 15:30–33. He hoped to win their favor and support for his projected labors in regions further west. When he set out on his last journey to Jerusalem, Paul said, "After I have gone there, I must also see Rome," Acts 19:21. He eventually got to Rome—but as a *prisoner*.

## THE KEY ISSUES

**1** **ILLUSTRATION 55A** helps define the central issues that dominate the contents of Paul's letter to the Romans:

   a. What constitutes the new people of God—God's **TRUE ISRAEL**?
   b. How does a person become a member of God's new people (***question mark***)?
   c. How does a person demonstrate ***discipleship within THE TRUE ISRAEL*** (*lower section*)?

Paul deals with questions 1a and 1b in Romans 1–11, and with question 1c in Romans 12–16.

**2** In answering the above questions, Paul points to two options:

   a. **Genetic links to Abraham, and the beliefs and practices of Judaism** (*top left*): Symbols for ***Abraham***, ***Sarah***, ***Isaac***; ***Hagar*** and ***Ishmael***; the ***land of Israel***; ***Sinai***, ***covenant***, ***community***; ***commandments*** and ***oral traditions***; ***Temple ground-plan***.
   b. **A faith relationship with Jesus the Messiah** (*top right*): ***manger***, ***Servant-King Jesus***; ***Jesus on cross***; ***open tomb***; ***arrow rising into cloud***.

Paul declares that fellowship with God is established by faith in the saving mission of the incarnate, crucified, risen, and ascended Jesus the Messiah.

**3** *Question mark; drop of water above center circle:* How does a person become a member of God's eternal, redeemed community? A person becomes a participant of Christ's saving work and a member of the true Israel through a "holy adoption process." In Holy Baptism, God declares those being baptized to be sharers in, and partakers of, all that Jesus the Messiah did and achieved; see **ILLUSTRATION 55D**.

**4** *Global community around Jesus, the Servant-King* (*lower section*): In all they think, say, and do, those who have been adopted into God's new people—whether Jew or Gentile—are to reflect the servant life of Jesus as they live out life in believing, praising, caring, and sharing community.

**55B**

**1** Sometimes the message of Romans is overly simplified to: People cannot save themselves by good deeds. They can be saved only by faith in Jesus who died for their sins and forgives them. Nothing else matters! **ILLUSTRATION 55B** sums up this view of things. (**ILLUSTRATION 55D** has more to say about this issue.)

> **Frame 1:** People become conscious of the **gulf** that sin has created between God and themselves, and of the death (**tombstone and skull**) that awaits them unless they do something about the sin that separates them from God.

> **Frame 2:** They set out to overcome that separation through good deeds. They look on obedience to **God's commandments** as a means of bridging the gulf between God and themselves.

> **Frame 3:** All efforts to establish a relationship with God through striving to obey God's commandments end in failure, death, and eternal death.

> **Frame 4:** God has already bridged the gulf between Himself and humanity. God comes to fallen humanity through **Jesus' cross ❶**, gathers people into fellowship with Himself, and bestows on them the joy of living in His eternal presence ❷.

**2** The role of Israel in divine history lay at the center of Paul's thinking. It formed the background of the heritage in which he had been reared. What role would *old Israel* play in the new people of God? To answer this, it was essential to define what constitutes the *true Israel*.

**3** Jewish teachers maintained that membership in God's people was established by obedience to the Law. Law was something more than the Ten Commandments. According to some, it was that body of law-codes contained in the first five books of Moses. According to others, it was the body of law-codes and traditions contained in all of the Old Testament books—and the oral traditions of the scribes and Pharisees as well.

**4** In the final analysis, the belief was that the ground for acceptance by God was conformity to legal precepts—a *merit system*. Gentiles desiring membership in God's people had to embrace the Mosaic Law, which meant that they had to convert to Judaism—and believe and live like Jews. To belong to God meant belonging to a specific people and conforming to that people's way of life.

**5** Paul dismisses this position. He asserts that God has no national favorites and is at work through Jesus to bring all people, whether Jew or Gentile ("everyone who has faith," 1:16), into one new community. No ritual or act of obedience, including circumcision, is of any value in establishing a relationship with God. Obedience is not a matter of observing ritual requirements, but a matter of responding in faith and trust to Jesus' saving and atoning mission.

**6** All humanity stands condemned before God, whether Jew or Gentile. The Jews know the will of God through the Law, but do not keep that Law—for no one can! The Gentiles know the will of God through conscience—the law of nature—but do not do what that law says. Both systems of Law show their adherents' sins, render them speechless before God, and show them to be subject to divine condemnation.

**7** God makes people, whether Jew or Gentile, right with Him wholly apart from any system of Law. God does it by grace. God always has and always will. God's grace is not vague and nebulous. It demonstrated itself in Jesus the Messiah who destroyed the power and authority of sin through His death and resurrection. To belong to Jesus (by acknowledging His saving, forgiving Lordship and submitting to His will) is to belong to the people of God, "the true Israel." Israel's role in the divine plan continues. However, the question of who belongs to "Israel" must be defined on the basis of allegiance to Christ.

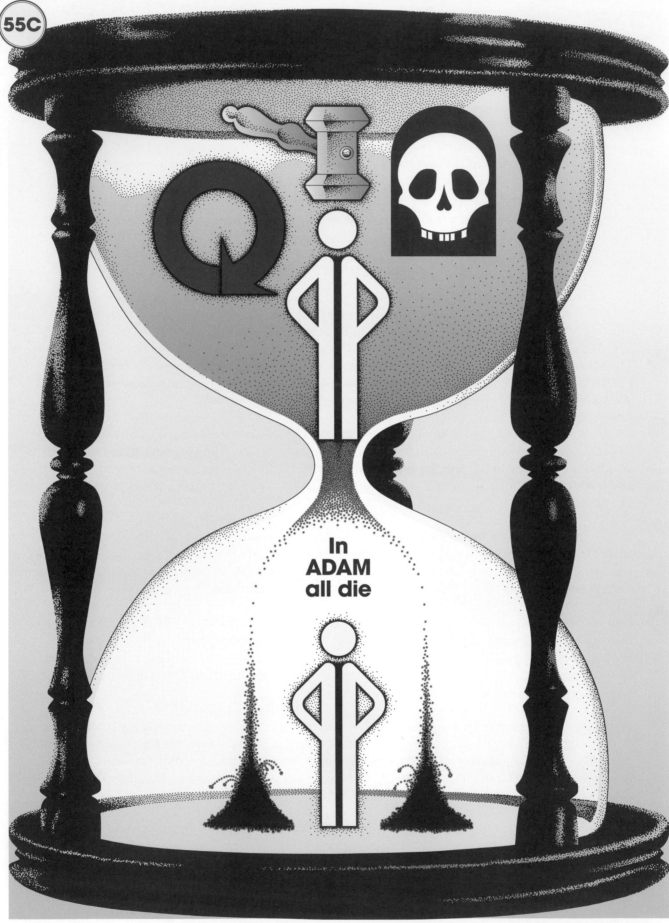

In
ADAM
all die

**1** Unit 8, *The Covenant at Sinai*, pointed out that the pivotal events in the life of ancient Israel took place when God rescued the Israelites from bondage in Egypt, took them to Mt. Sinai, and made a covenant with them. Through the centuries that followed, successive generations linked themselves inseparably to those events, Deuteronomy 26:5–9. They saw themselves as part of a *privileged* community rather than as part of a *fallen* humanity.

**2** As the postexilic period unfolded, Jewish teachers taught that only true descendants of Abraham could belong to the people of God, and only they would take part in the events of the age to come, Ezra 2:59–63, 10:6–17; Nehemiah 13:23–27. They said that the Law, or *Torah*, was the first thing created. It was the blueprint on which creation was established, and all Jews were required to keep it. Although the rabbinic school of Shammai denied Gentiles any part in the world to come, the school of Hillel showed a more gracious attitude and said that they could take part in the world to come if they kept the commandments given to Noah; see Acts 15:28,29.

*Rabbi Shammai* was a native of Judea. *Rabbi Hillel* came to Jerusalem from Babylon where there was still a Jewish community with schools for studying the Hebrew Scriptures—the Torah in particular. Shammai and Hillel gave so many conflicting decisions when interpreting the Torah that they created two schools, the strict "House of Shammai" and the moderate "House of Hillel." After the destruction of Jerusalem in A.D. 70, the House of Hillel gained ascendancy.

**3** While respecting the memory and significance of the exodus events for his fellow Jews, Paul went further back in time and linked the whole of humanity, including the Jewish people, to Adam, Romans 5:12–19. Although the ancient Israelites and Jews could say, "The history of the patriarchs is my history. I was there. I participated!" Paul could say, "Adam's history is our history. The human race, including all Jews, took part in the fall into sin in Eden. By birth, all humanity is 'in Adam.'"

**4** **ILLUSTRATION 55C** *sums up Paul's message in relation to humanity being "in Adam."*

    a. *Upper section* of **hourglass:** The person is **Adam**. Above him are symbols for *sin* (**circular arrow**), *judgment* (**gavel**), and *death and condemnation* (**tombstone and skull**).

    b. *Lower section* of **hourglass: The sands of Adam's history flow into the present, surround humanity today, and link all people to Adam's sin and its consequences.** Our history is linked inseparably to Adam's history.

**5** Paul's awareness of sharing in Adam's plight caused him to cry out, "Wretched man that I am! Who will rescue me from this body of death?" Romans 7:24. Paul points to the only effective answer when he writes:

> *For since death came through a human being, the resurrection of the dead has also come through a human being; for as all die in Adam, so all will be made alive in Christ.*
> (1 Corinthians 15:21,22)

**6** While Paul acknowledged that God had bestowed numerous honors on those descended from Abraham, he insisted that the ultimate problem is humanity's link to Adam. **ILLUSTRATION 55D** depicts his answer to the problem.

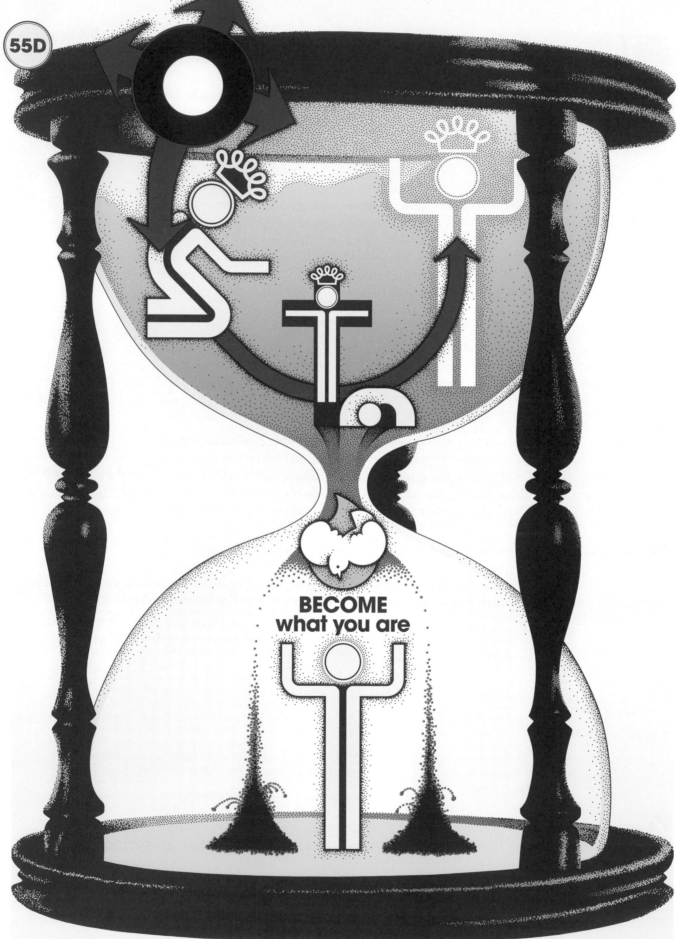

**1** The spiritual song asks, "Were you there when they crucified my Lord?" It expects the answer, "Yes! I saw it happen!" Paul assures God's people that they did not merely *watch* the crucifixion. By virtue of their baptism, they *shared in* and *experienced* it. He writes:

> *For surely you know that when we were baptized into union with Christ Jesus, we were baptized into union with His death. By our baptism, then, we were buried with Him and shared His death, in order that just as Christ was raised from death by the glorious power of the Father, so we also might live a new life.* (Romans 6:3,4, TEV translation; see also Romans 6:5–8.)

By virtue of our physical birth, we share *in Adam* (**ILLUSTRATION 55C**). By virtue of our second birth in baptism, we share *in Jesus*.

**2** **ILLUSTRATION 55D**, *upper section* of **hourglass:** God sent Jesus to live the servant life (***Servant-King*** Jesus) we were meant to live but cannot, and to die the death (***cross***) we deserve to die so that we need not! Jesus broke the power of death (***open tomb***), rose triumphant from the grave (***rising arrow***), and remains among us today (***risen, glorified Jesus***).

**3** **ILLUSTRATION 55D**, *lower section* of **hourglass:** Through the waters of baptism (***drop of water*** in neck of hourglass), the Holy Spirit (***dove***) makes us partakers of, sharers in, all that Jesus has accomplished. When Jesus led a sinless life, we led it with Him. When Jesus was put to death to suffer the punishment for humanity's sin, we shared that death with Him. When Jesus was placed into the grave that sin brings, we went into that grave with Him. When Jesus rose triumphant from the grave, we shared that victory over death with Him; see also Ephesians 2:5,6.

**4** In Jesus, God gathered the human race into one Person. God let that one Person be what He intended the human race to be, and suffer what the human race deserved to suffer. In Holy Baptism, God declares us to have shared in all that Jesus lived, suffered, endured, and conquered. God incorporates us into Jesus' saving ministry and mission.

**5** Our "saving credentials" are not of *our making*, but of *God's giving*. When we stand before God on the Last Day of history, we shall point only to what God has given us. While we wait for that Last Day, God's appeal is: "***BECOME what you are***. Seek to make the credentials I have given you in grace describe you personally more and more. Seek to demonstrate in your own life what you have been given. Show your link to My Son Jesus. Live out what I have declared you to be."

**6** In summary: Our *problem link* is that to Adam. Our *saving link* is that to Christ. The commandments given at Sinai are not our guidelines for life; they were given to those who took part in the Exodus and their descendants—and had authority only until Jesus came, Galatians 3:24–26. Rather, we are to reflect the life of the Servant-King to whom we are inseparably and eternally linked. We are to make visible the invisible Jesus. As we shall see, the issues dealt with in relation to **ILLUSTRATIONS 55C** and **ILLUSTRATIONS 55D** lie at the very heart of Paul's letter to the Romans.

The following summarizes the thrust of Paul's theology in his letter to the Romans.

*Corinth, Greece*

*Dear beloved saints of God in Rome,*

*I am Paul, a slave of Jesus Christ. God has made me His ambassador to proclaim good news about His Son. This good news is not of recent origin, but was planned a long time ago, and proclaimed by the prophets. It is about the Kingdom of God as realized in the life, death, and resurrection of Jesus the Messiah, God's Son. Insofar as He was a man, He was a descendant of David. His resurrection from the dead through the Holy Spirit's power declares Him also to be God's Son, and our Lord. God has appointed apostles to proclaim the truth about Jesus to all nations, so that people everywhere might believe in Him. And so I greet you. Grace and peace to you from God our Father, and the Lord Jesus Christ.*

*Your faith is spoken of throughout the world, and I praise God for that. God knows that I pray about you regularly, and I ask God to make it possible for me to visit you. I long to share insights about God's Word. I would love to be able to reap a harvest of souls for Christ also in Rome.*

*When I come, my message will be the Gospel of Jesus Christ—nothing else. I am not ashamed of that truth, for it is God's power to bring both Jew and Greek to saving faith. Christ's Gospel reveals the divine righteousness that saves a person. The person who lays hold of it through faith is righteous before God, and lives victoriously and eternally.*

*We all need Christ. Apart from Him, all we can produce of ourselves is unrighteousness—and that arouses God to anger. Some will ask, "How can the heathen be expected to be in a right relationship with God? They don't even know Him!" Note that God has left His signature throughout creation. If only people would open their eyes and read it; but they don't, and, therefore, they can't blame God for the fate that awaits them. When people ignore God, darkness fills their minds. They claim to be wise, but are fools. They even make "gods" for themselves, and worship and serve them! They give God up, and God gives them up—with the result that their perverse minds plunge them into foul deeds that tear apart the relationship between God and people, and among people. The tragic truth is that, although they know the result of such behavior, they plunge themselves into it with gusto—and rejoice to see others do the same.* (Read Romans 1)

*Maybe some protest, "I don't do those vile things!" Wait! Isn't it true that you do? And if you do, don't you face the same judgment? Or do you prefer to presume on God's mercy, and assume that God will turn a blind eye to just you alone? God's mercy has a goal—to move us to repent. God has no pets, no favorites. Being a Jew does not entitle one to special treatment. On the last day, God will treat all persons of all nations precisely as they deserve to be treated.*

*Jews may boast, "We have the Law!" Fine! But it is one thing to **have** the Law, and another to **heed** and **do** it. The Gentiles may not have the Jewish Law, but they have their own moral codes and a conscience. All stand condemned before God for no one obeys those laws perfectly.*

*If you feel smug because you are a Jew, because you are a member of the chosen people, because you possess the Law, and because you are in a position to instruct ignorant pagans, let me ask you: **Do you keep the law?** You decry stealing, but do you steal? You condemn adultery, but are you sexually pure? You attack pagan idol worship, but do you rob temples? Surely you know that Gentiles look at Jewish behavior and maintain they want nothing of the Jewish God! Yet you boast about being members of the covenant people and being circumcised. What good is your circumcision if your deeds don't ratify it? Uncircumcised pagans—if they are obedient— please God more than disobedient Jews do. What matters is obedience—not some bodily mark.* (Read ch. 2)

*Perhaps some are asking what advantage there is to being a Jew—that special people God has blessed so richly. The advantages are many. God has given them His truth. Fortunately, Jewish faithlessness does not*

invalidate God's faithfulness. Never argue that if God is angry with you, He can't be just. That argument is wrong. If you suggest that you might as well sin to give God more opportunity to forgive, you are playing with words. Although grace abounds in God's heart, God is also your **judge**. Don't forget that.

Jews stand on the same level before God as Gentiles, for they are all equally under the dominion of sin. Many passages in the sacred writings point out how sin has thoroughly infected our total being, our throat, tongue, lips, mouth, feet, and eyes. No person on earth does what is right and walks in God's paths.

If you think that there is anything about your life that moves God to like and accept you, you are wrong. God's Law exposes us for what we are. It tells us to shut our boasting mouths before God. Our actions do not make us **acceptable to** God, but **accountable before** God. God accepts no one on the basis of supposed "good deeds." The more we study God's Law, the more we find out how corrupt we are in God's sight.

However, although we can do nothing to make ourselves right with God, He has provided a solution. Although we have no righteousness of our own to offer to God, **God gives us a righteousness that we can offer to Him**. God talks about it in detail in our scriptures. This "saving righteousness" is what God has done for us through His Son, Jesus the Messiah. Incredibly, although no one on earth is better than anyone else (we have all sinned and failed to do what God wants), God has declared us all "just" before Him. God gives us a new status before Him— note, "gives." It's all grace. How does this work? Well, although God is certainly angry about sin, He provided a Substitute to take the place of the guilty party, of humanity itself! That's the "good news"! Jesus has suffered what we deserve—our death, judgment, and punishment. It is as though Jesus appears before the Judge and says, "Father, forgive them for My sake. I obeyed Your will perfectly. I have suffered what the sinful world deserves. Don't look at their sin. Look at my righteousness." The amazing thing is that the Judge wants it this way, and asks us, "Do **you** want it this way? Do **you** accept this gift that I want to give you, or do **you** still want to go it alone and do it **your** way?"

God does not want us to prepare a package of good works to give Him to persuade Him to love and accept us. We must remain empty-handed before God. God has prepared the necessary gift for us, offers it to each of us, and begs us to take it. That's truly good news for you. God gives what He demands—and God does all this for His enemies!

Obviously, we are dealing with a divine principle. All human boasting is ruled out. Everything depends on what God has done for us in Christ. We humans merely receive by faith what God gives. God's gift makes us right before Him—nothing else. The same principle applies to Jews and Gentiles. (Read ch. 3)

No doubt some ask, "Has it always been that way? What about Abraham?" Well, what about Abraham? Nothing Abraham **did** made him God's child. Remember what our scriptures say? "Abraham **believed** God, and it was **reckoned** to him as righteousness." (Do remember that David stressed that blessedness before God consists in being **forgiven** by God.)

When was righteousness "reckoned" to Abraham? Before or after circumcision? **Before** he was circumcised! Being circumcised did not contribute to his becoming God's child. His circumcision served simply as a bodily mark stating that he was righteous before God because of a divine promise that was his through faith. He is, therefore, the "father" of all who are righteous before God through faith, even though they have never been circumcised as he was—even as he is also the "father" of his descendants who trust for salvation in the same promise that he did. God did not make promises to Abraham on the basis of a merit system. If salvation is based on merit, then it is not "by grace, through faith." However, it **is** all by promise and grace, through faith. Abraham persisted in trusting God's promises even when, from a human point of view, everything seemed impossible. Although people are weak, God is not.

We, too, need to be people of faith like Abraham and trust only in what God has done for us through His Son, Jesus the Messiah. Jesus died for us, in our stead. The punishment we deserve was placed on Jesus. God raised Him from the dead to declare a loud, "**Yes!**" to all that Jesus did, and to assure us that what Jesus did avails for us also. That alone is to be the basis of our trust. (Read ch. 4)

What God has done for us in Jesus creates a new relationship between God and us. We don't have to spend life trying to make God love and accept us—a futile action! God has declared us just before Him. What peace that brings! Even so, life will not necessarily be a bed of roses. That does not matter, for whatever comes our way, we can be filled with inner joy and hope. God is for us! Whatever difficulties we encounter can serve to make us more what God would have us be.

Do take to heart the incredible fact that God did not do all these wonderful things for **good** people, but for **sinners**—for His **enemies**! If God has made us His now, we can be sure that He will save us from any future wrath or judgment. God has solved our whole problem in relation to sin—in time and for eternity! What joy there is in knowing this!

Sin began when Adam did what he was forbidden to do, and his sin infects everyone who descended from him—and that's the human race. It is true that the Law was not given until Sinai, and that (strictly speaking) there was no set of laws in existence from Adam to Moses. One is not conscious of having sinned where there is no law to point out what one should and should not do. However, sin pervaded the human scene from Adam to Moses because Adam was, in a real sense, **every person**. Everyone alive has a solidarity with Adam: his sin, his guilt, and his death. Descent from Adam accomplishes this. We all belong to "Adam's clan," and share what our ancestor was and what he brought on himself.

The good news is that God sent a Second Adam, God's Son, Jesus the Messiah. Jesus accomplished something completely different for the human race. Through Jesus' achievement, God makes available to humanity obedience, righteousness, acquittal, peace, grace, forgiveness, and eternal life. All this is offered as a gift, to be received in faith. **The first Adam brought only tragedy to humanity; the Second Adam brings only joy and blessing to humanity.** (Read ch. 5)

There is still that warped suggestion that says, "One might as well sin as much as possible to give God more opportunity to forgive." How can anyone want to continue to serve sin when he has died to its power, authority, and control? What I mean is this: Your baptism severed all ties with your former "director of life." Why, then, have anything to do with what the power of sin suggests?

Remember what happened in your baptism. Jesus gave you His sinless life to possess as though you yourself had lived it. When He died on the cross, you were on the cross sharing His death. You went into the grave with Him. When He rose from the dead and left the grave that is punishment for sin once and for all, you rose with Him. In fact, in rising with Him, you entered the realm of eternity itself.

Why, then, serve your old master, the power of sin? Serve your New Master, Jesus the Messiah. You don't have to worry about being good enough for God to accept you. God already has accepted you. You are now free to devote life to saying, "Thank You" to Him for justifying and accepting you. Imagine! God has declared you to be holy—a saint! God now simply asks that you try to become what He has declared you to be: "holy." Your old master pays horrendous wages—death! Your New Master pays no wages, but just lavishes everything, including eternal life, on you as a gift. (Read ch. 6)

The grand truth is that, in our baptism, we died to all obligation to try to keep the Law as a means of persuading God to accept us. The Law has no authority to demand that of us anymore. It is no longer our master. Jesus is! We are now free to serve God for the right reasons.

Maybe some of you are thinking, "God gave us the Law, and because God is good, the Law must be good. Paul, are you suggesting that the Law is bad?" No! The **Law** is **good**; **people** are **bad**. They are sinners, and have only themselves to blame for their condition. God's good Law simply shows sinful people how bad they really are. It enables people to see themselves as God sees them.

The problem lies in people, not in the Law. They put the Law to a wrong use—as a merit system to persuade God to accept them. That's blindness! Even worse, there is that Satanic streak in humanity that says, "Rules

*were meant to be broken." The result is that, when God's Law says, "Don't do that!" people do the wrong thing just because it is forbidden. The irony is that, when people come into contact with God's **good** Law, they do that which is **bad**. How perverse we are!*

*There are times when I personally do not feel any real sense of sin. Then I come into contact with the Law, and am reminded about right and wrong. I then set out to do what the Law asks, only to find that I cannot. A profound sense of sin rises up within me. (The evil is in **me**, not in the **Law**.) I set out to do right, but find myself doing wrong. I agree that the Law's command is right, and that I should do what it says—but find myself doing the opposite, doing the very things I hate. What a plight! Is there any way out of this impossible situation? There is, thank God—in Jesus the Messiah.* (Read ch. 7)

*God's good news declares that there is no condemnation for those in Christ Jesus. When the Holy Spirit brings us into fellowship with Christ, He frees us from the realm of sin and death, and the tyranny that goes with it. The Law cannot produce a right relationship with God. It cannot give us the necessary vitality for proper obedience. The good that the Law might accomplish is undone by what is in us—the power of sin that dominates us.*

*But God has acted to overcome the power of sin. God came in a form like ours in the person of Jesus, only without sin, and took upon Himself the effects of what sin does to people. He resisted the power of sin. He permitted it no dominion over His life at all. He endured death and went into the grave that sin brings. He suffered the curse that the Law brings about. He then conquered death and rose from the grave. In our baptism, He permits us to share a solidarity with all that He achieved.*

*Although the Law tells people how to live, it gives them no power to do what it asks.*

*Things are different for those in Christ. His Spirit supplies the necessary power to do God's will. Although our perverse inner nature still wants to live only for the sake of self, God works to change the situation. God acts through the Spirit to create peace between Himself and us. The Spirit takes up residence in us and directs our conduct. We are under new management, as it were. Had God left us to ourselves, we could never have coped with the confusion, conflict, and muddled motives that surface in us when we come face to face with the Law. Had God not intervened, we would have remained rebellious sinners—at war with God. Now that we are in Christ, all is new and different. Let us make use of the Spirit's power to keep Christ enthroned in our lives.*

*Just think! Because of Christ, we are now God's "children." Not slaves, but children—who can address God as "Daddy." We are also heirs of all that is God's. God's true Son, Jesus the Messiah, shares all that belongs to His Father.*

*True, there will be suffering in this world. Suffering goes hand-in-hand with earthly life. However, suffering is only a short-term affair on the way to glory. Even creation itself longs for the time when it will be freed from the corruption, pollution, and bondage that swept in when humanity sinned. No matter what we might have to endure in this life, the Spirit has already made us God's children. Therefore, we can certainly look forward to sharing the full harvest of glory when this life ends. This kind of hope empowers us to cope with anything in this life, and to give a lively witness to the world around us. We are never alone. The Spirit walks beside us to help and encourage us. He knows the unspoken longings that rise in our hearts. He can read our sighs.*

*Never forget that God accomplishes good in and through everything that happens to us. God's every action is directed to bringing about the final glory of those who trust in Christ. During life on this side of the grave, God wants to reproduce in us the image of His Son by progressively sharing with us the risen life of Jesus Himself.*

*Who, then, can be against us? God? God has already pronounced sentence in our favor. There is no reason to think God plans to act differently. What about Jesus? He reminds the Father of all our needs and intercedes for us continually. Who, then, can separate us from the love that Jesus has for us? No one! Nothing! Troubles that touch us do not indicate that God has stopped loving us. In every situation, we are victors and conquerors.*

*Nothing can cut us off from the love God has for us in Christ Jesus, our Lord. Death can't. Life can't. No supernatural being can. No astrological power can. **We are God's forever!*** (Read ch. 8)

# God Still Has a People, an Israel

**55F**

**1** Paul's discourse in chs. 1–8 serves as the basis for chs. 9–11, where he struggles with Israel's persistent unbelief and continuing rejection of Jesus. Israel's action is tragic, for God specifically prepared it for the coming of the Messiah. The situation causes Paul intense grief. He would sacrifice his own salvation if it meant that Israel would come to faith, 9:1–5.

**2** Israel's error is that it assumes salvation to be a matter of heredity and national privilege. It is not! Both Sarah (through Hagar and Ishmael) and Rebekah (who bore Jacob and Esau) sought to intervene in the divine plan, only to find that God achieves His purposes His way through individuals He chooses in grace. God can, if He so desires, raise up a Moses to bless—and a pharaoh to be the object of wrath, 9:6–18. In all this, humanity has no cause to accuse God of favoritism or injustice. As the creator and Lord of the universe, God can use the seemingly unworthy to achieve His larger goals. People dare not argue with God as though they are on the same level as He is, 9:19–24.

**3** God still has a people. God has been reaping a rich harvest among the Gentiles. Those who were once "far off" have responded to Christ in faith, while those who were "near" (Old Israel) have rejected God. Their rejection of Christ stems from their insistence that salvation is a matter of conformity to legal principles and ritual observance. In rejecting Christ, Israel does precisely what the Old Testament prophets predicted it would do, 9:25–33.

**4** Indeed, old Israel remains zealous for God, but its zeal is based on a false principle—obedience to Law. Christ put an end to Law as a saving instrument. Fellowship with Christ is established by faith—regardless of moral achievement or ethnic origins, 10:1–13. God proclaimed this saving principle to Israel throughout its history. Although Israel heard it, Israel responded in unbelief—even as it does today, 10:14–21.

**5** However, not all Jews have rejected Christ. Paul's own experience is a witness to that. Other Jews—admittedly a remnant minority—have come to faith. Israel's present rejection does not mean that it will remain obstinate forever. The divine irony is that, as a result of Israel's refusal to come to faith, the Gentiles have been gathered in, 11:1–12. If Israel's unbelief led to that, greater things will result from Israel's return to faith, 11:13–16. Indeed, Israel remains precious in God's sight, which is evident in the "first fruits" it has produced from the patriarchs to the present "remnant." The Gentiles should learn from Israel's unbelief lest they repeat its error. Israel grew out of the original "stump" of God's people. The Gentiles have other origins; they have merely been grafted into God's original stump. If the Gentiles could be effectively grafted into that stump (to which they had no previous connection), Israel is surely more ready to sprout and grow when grafted back into its own original stump, 11:17–24.

**6** Israel's rejection of the Gospel is only temporary. The nation will not remain blind, but will return to God's true family after the Gentiles have come to faith. The paradox is that Israel became disobedient so that the Gentiles might receive mercy—and that Israel might eventually receive mercy once again. Why does God work this way? God's ways are beyond understanding. Mere humans must simply bow before God in praise and adoration—and leave it at that, 11:25–36.

**1** The members of the new community observe a new worship style in that they offer God their very bodies (rather than animals) as "sacrifices." They avoid any temptations to conform to the standards of the world order around them, and in all things demonstrate publicly God's will for His people, 12:1,2. The members are to interrelate to one another as parts of a single body. Each person is to have only one goal—to glorify God by serving others within the community, 12:3–21.

**2** Members of the new people are to reflect their relationship with Christ to those outside the "body" as well as to those within it—for example, in their stance toward political authority. They are to pay their taxes and give due respect to government leaders. Government exists to maintain order and to protect those within its realm, 13:1–7. God's people are not to be social revolutionaries, but are to live in quiet obedience. They are to demonstrate understanding toward fellow-Christians on matters of diet and other items of personal preference, 14:1–15:21.

**3** In the concluding section (15:22–16:27), Paul greets friends in Rome and outlines future hopes and plans.

**55A** Paul wrote his letter to the Romans while in Corinth toward the end of his third missionary journey. He wanted to prepare the Roman church for his coming visit in the course of his travels to Spain. He hoped that the Roman Christians would speed him on his way there. In the body of the letter, Paul stresses that the Gospel is the power of God for salvation, because it is the revelation of the righteousness of God through faith.

In this letter, Paul raises the question: "What establishes a relationship with God and membership in His Kingdom?"

● Genetic links to the patriarchs? Living within the borders of the Holy Land? Seeking to obey the commandments given at Mt. Sinai, and the oral traditions revealed at Mt. Sinai? Offering the appropriate sacrifice in the Jerusalem Temple?

● Or: Being adopted into Gods' eternal family through Holy Baptism—an adoptive act through which one is declared a participant in Jesus' sinless life, atoning death, and victory over death?

Paul says "Yes!" to the second option. At the same time, he exhorts his readers to give much thought to the implications of being adopted into God's eternal family. They are to live in community, reflecting Jesus' mind, manner, and ministry in all their dealings with one another.

**55B** Our so-called "saintly efforts" do not establish a relationship with God. They merely reflect the relationship God has established with us. They do not bring us into God's presence. Rather, they reflect the joyous truth that God has gathered us into His presence.

**55C** Although, in Paul's day, many looked to their involvement in the Exodus from Egypt (as the Jews understood the concept of "remembering the past"), Paul reminds his readers that their "memory link" does not go back far enough. All humanity, including the Jewish people, has links to Adam— and share involvement in Adam's sin, judgment, and death.

**55D** However, that was not Paul's "final word." Those who have been baptized into Christ (God's Second Adam) share His sinless life, His death as a consequence of sin, and His victory over death and the grave. They have already been declared citizens of the life to come—and are to seek to live *now* as they will *then* when they finally enter God's Eternal Home.

**55E** Paul's letter to the Romans is detailed and profound. The key points that surface within it are:

● Although all people are unrighteous and subject to the wrath of God, God has made a saving righteousness available through the work of Christ. It is offered to all as a gracious gift, to be laid hold of through faith.

● This saving righteousness is bestowed in Holy Baptism. It frees those who receive it from the futility of seeking salvation through obedience to Jewish laws—or any law. God has given believers righteousness as a gift. Because God has *declared them holy* in Christ, they are free to seek to *become what they are*: a holy people who already possess eternal life.

● God has been righteous in all His dealings with Israel—which has only itself to blame for its exclusion from the Kingdom of God.

● Those who possess the gift of salvation in Christ are to live a life of loving service toward one another and those outside their community.

**55F** Those whom God has made members of His new community are to see themselves involved in a non-stop "sacrificial process" of offering life to the glory of God in the service of others. Among other things, they are to reflect their relationship to God by honoring those with political authority, in matters of diet, and in all other issues relating to the use of life.

# CROSS WAYS®

**6 SECTION**

**UNITS 51–60**

## The Letters and Revelation

## UNIT 56
### The Captivity Letters

*Letters from Paul in Prison*

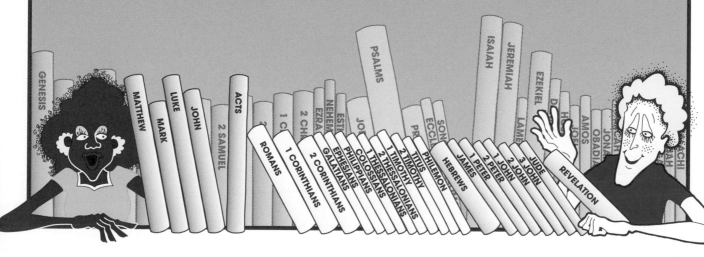

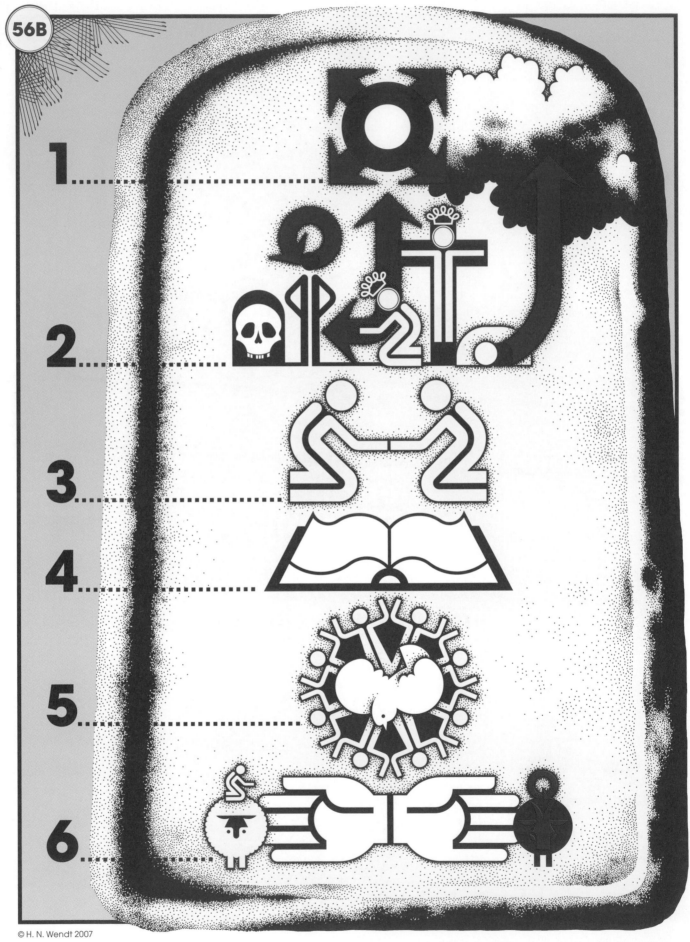

1 ......................................................

2 ......................................................

3 ......................................................

4 ......................................................

5 ......................................................

6 ......................................................

After completing his third missionary journey, Paul followed his usual practice of visiting Jerusalem. When a Jewish mob attacked him, Roman authorities took him into protective custody and transferred him to a prison in Caesarea. After several years in confinement, Paul appealed for his case to be heard by Caesar in Rome. To Rome and Caesar he went. During his two-year imprisonment in Rome, Paul was not reduced to total inactivity. He had his own lodgings, and his friends and coworkers were permitted to visit him, Acts 28:30. Paul did not limit his witness to personal contacts in Rome. He wrote letters to minister to others further afield. The four letters listed below, traditionally referred to as the "Captivity Letters," are ascribed to this period.

a. **Ephesians**, which defines the nature and life of the Church.

b. **Colossians**, which proclaims Jesus the Messiah's cosmic significance.

c. **Philippians**, which encourages a suffering church to wait with expectant joy.

d. **Philemon**, which gives insights into how God's Good News (Gospel) can transform a life.

The order in which these four letters were written is debated. Ephesians and Colossians are very similar in content; comments made about some of the passages in Ephesians apply equally well to many passages in Colossians.

# Because I—Therefore You

**ILLUSTRATION 8C** analyzed the structure of the covenant God made with Israel at Sinai. In the first two sections of that covenant formulation, God tells the people *who He is* and *what He has done for them* (**God's Indicatives**). In the third section, God tells the people *how they are to respond to His grace and goodness* by obeying His commandments (**God's Imperatives**).

**ILLUSTRATION 56B** depicts the New Testament counterpart of the Sinai covenant. Its thought patterns underlie Paul's appeals to his readers (in particular, sections 1–3). It can be understood as follows:

**1** **Preamble**

"Blessed be the God and Father of our Lord Jesus Christ," Ephesians 1:3.

**2** **Historical Prologue**

"who has blessed us in Christ with every spiritual blessing," Ephesians 1:3–6; see also Romans 4:25 and Romans 8.

**3** **Commandments** (or **Stipulations**)

Ephesians 4:17–6:20; Colossians 3:1–4:6; Romans 12:1–15:6.

**4** **Preservation and Re-reading**

Ephesians 5:19,20; Colossians 3:16.

**5** **Witnesses**

Romans 8:16

**6** **Blessings and curses**

Romans 4:6–8, 14:22,23; Galatians 3:9–13; Ephesians 1:3.

The "Because I (God)—therefore you (My People)" pattern is particularly evident in Ephesians. In the first three chapters of Ephesians, Paul states who God is and describes what He has done for the salvation of humanity. In the final three chapters, Paul defines the impact that God's grace in Christ is to have on the life of individual believers, and on the life of the Christian community as a whole.

56C

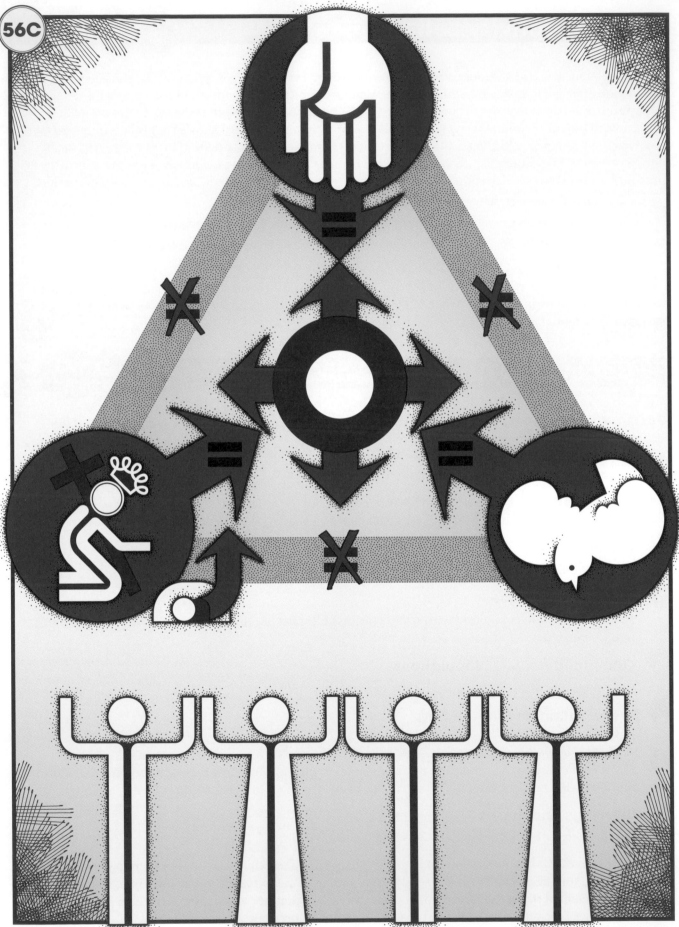

**1** Ephesus was a large seaport on the western coast of Asia Minor, a Roman province. Paul spent time there during his *second* missionary journey (Acts 18:19–21) and made it his base during his *third* missionary journey, spending about three years there, Acts 19:1–20:1. It is unusual that the letter contains only one personal reference—to Tychicus, Ephesians 6:21; see Colossians 4:7. Indications are that Ephesians was initially a circular letter designed for a wider distribution. The title, "To the Ephesians," was probably not in the original letter; it is missing in the most reliable ancient manuscripts.

**2** Ephesians is a letter in form only. It is actually a theological treatise. The first three chapters deal with doctrine, and outline what God has done for the redemption of the universe. The final three chapters instruct God's sons and daughters how to respond to His initiative and to live as His children. This sequence is important, for it declares that the Christian life is a *response to what God has already done* for the salvation of humanity.

**3** After the opening greeting and salutation (1:1,2), chs. 1–3 set forth God's great plan, hidden since the beginning of the world, to make Jesus the Messiah the Head of a new family of humanity—a family that will embrace both Jew and Gentile. In chs. 4–6, Paul outlines the good works God's new creation, the church, is to perform. The following comments help crystallize Paul's message.

**4** **ILLUSTRATION 56C** (*upper section*) depicts the message of Ephesians 1:3–14. In the original Greek, the section is one long sentence. (The RSV and NRSV translations break down this one Greek sentence into six sentences.) Its expressions literally tumble over one another as they summon the reader to join in praising the One "who accomplishes all things according to His counsel and will," 1:11. This opening overture is made up of three sections that deal, in turn, with the work of:

    a. The Father, vv. 3–6 (*top circle*, **Creator's hand**): The Father designed the plan for the universe.

    b. The Son, vv. 7–12 (*left circle*, **Jesus as Servant-King, cross, open tomb, rising arrow**): The Son is the One through whom God put the plan into effect.

    c. The Holy Spirit, vv. 13,14 (*right circle*, **dove**): The Spirit is the guarantee that God's people will finally receive the eternal inheritance that is the goal of God's work in liberating humanity.

On **each arrow** from **each Person** to the **symbol for God** in the *center* is an **"equals"** sign, indicating that each Person of the Trinity is, in turn, fully God. On the **speckled lines** flowing from **Father** to **Son** to **Holy Spirit** is an **"equals"** sign **cancelled out**, indicating that the Father is not the Son, and the Son is not the Spirit, and the Spirit is not the Father.

**5** **ILLUSTRATION 56C** (*lower section*): Each section concludes with a summons to *praise*, 1:6,12,14. When Paul refers to the Trinity, he does not concern himself with how there can be three Persons in one God. Rather, he summons all creation to praise that one God who acted in love and forgiving grace for the salvation of humanity.

**6** Ephesians takes in the total sweep of redemptive history. Paul begins his presentation with a statement about God's decision "before the foundation of the world" (1:4), and carries it forward through "the fullness of time" (1:10) to that moment when, at the end of our present history, the Lordship of Jesus the Messiah will embrace all things in heaven and on earth, 1:20–23. Throughout his letter, Paul bids his readers to be on guard against having a God who is too small.

**7** The key thought occurs in 1:9,10. In these two verses, the apostle declares that the universe is not some accidental structure stumbling along on its own, and history is not just one fool thing after another. God is at work in the *universe* (that He made and owns) and in *history* according to His good pleasure. God has a plan for the universe and everything in it. God's plan is no secret; He has made it public. God is at work to bring about an ultimate unity and harmony of all created things in Jesus the Messiah.

**8** God has not only told humanity about His plan; He has involved them in it. The Church is the instrument through which God is at work to achieve His plan. The Church is to be a microcosm, a display in miniature, of God's original plan for the universe. Even "the rulers and authorities in the heavenly places" are finding what this plan is by looking at what is going on in the Church, 3:10.

**9** God's love is not motivated by anything lovable in what He sees. God acts in grace to make spiritually alive those who are spiritually dead in trespasses and sins, 2:1. This death does not have to do with cold, rigid bodies—for human hearts, minds, and limbs are very much alive with activity. However, this activity is not in response to God's love and will, but in response to "the course of this world," "the ruler of the power of the air" (2:2), and the passions of "flesh." Before God intervenes in our lives, we heed the whims of body and mind, and, like the rest of humanity, are subject to God's wrath and judgment, 2:2,3. We are separated from God, not numbered among the people of God, without hope in the world, and "far off," 2:12,13.

**10** God has acted to change all that. He has blessed, chosen, and rescued us, destined us to be His children, lavished His grace on us, revealed His gracious will to us, and appointed us to live for the praise of His glory, 1:3–14. God has enlightened our hearts (1:18) and worked in us with mighty power, 1:19. God has made us alive in Christ, 2:5–7. God accomplished all through Christ and offers all in Christ. Paul uses expressions like "in Christ" nine times in 1:3–14. He wants to be sure that no one misses the point!

**11** Paul wants his readers to remember that Jesus' ministry in relation to procuring their salvation was no easy affair. It involved pain, humiliation, and the shedding of blood, 1:7. The only way humanity could be set free from its hatred of God, and its bondage to sin, was by the sacrifice of the one Divine Life. We are saved by Christ's blood—there are no "ifs" or "buts" about this. Humanity shrinks from this "blood language" because it fails to understand that people, as they are born into this world, are in open revolt against the Creator. God sent His Son to Calvary to offer forgiveness to those who could offer only sin to Him.

**12** God's greatest redemptive act took place when He raised Jesus from the dead, 1:18–20. That act was the pivotal point of history, and a demonstration of God's limitless power and might. After God raised Jesus from the dead, He "seated Jesus at His right hand in the heavenly places," 1:20,21. This means that the Father has entrusted to His Son the task of running the universe. Throughout its billions of galaxies, throughout its billions of suns and planets, Christ is Lord. He has been given the power and authority to rule all things. The imagery used in this verse probably stems from the ancient practice of representing a king as seated next to the god of a city or nation. To occupy the right hand of a god meant that the ruler exercised power in the name of, and on behalf of, his god.

**13** In 1:22, Paul writes, God "has put all things under His feet." The imagery of putting enemies under one's feet is derived from the ancient practice of having the faces or figures of a nation's vanquished opponents woven or engraved on the footstool of its conquering king. Paul uses this picture to

point out that Christ is already Lord, that all His enemies have been conquered, and that, as history proceeds, they are being made subject to Him.

**14** God appointed Jesus as Head over all things "for the Church, which is His body," 1:22,23. Paul uses the term "body" to declare that, in some mysterious way, the Church is to be an extension of its Lord. It is to carry on His work. It is His instrument to carry out His mission of gathering all things under Jesus' Lordship. The Church is not something spiritual and invisible that hovers above life and society. It is that representative body of Jesus the Messiah that God has created to work among people with all their burdens, tragedies, and frustrations.

**15** God is at work through the Church to cut across all boundaries of race and culture and to gather all people around His Son's throne. In Paul's day, God accomplished the remarkable feat of breaking down the barrier that separated Jew and Gentile—God did away with the "dividing wall" of the Mosaic Law with its multitude of regulations. Both Jew and Gentile (that is, all people) are now to look to the teachings and example of Jesus the Messiah for direction in life. Through Jesus' cross, all have access to the Father. And in the servanthood to which Jesus summons them lies the only hope of unity and harmony among humanity. Only in Jesus is there hope of putting the human race back together again, 2:11–19.

**16** The Church is God's new dwelling place, His new Temple. The Servant Christ is its Cornerstone; He alone determines its shape and form. The prophets and apostles proclaimed the truth about Christ, and were the first ones gathered into God's New Temple. They form its foundation. As time proceeds, God adds more and more living stones to this "structure" and desires to mold each one to match the servant-shape of Jesus the Messiah, 2:19–22. (See also **ILLUSTRATION 53A**.)

**17** The "therefore" of Ephesians 4:1, and the contents of the three chapters that follow, remind us that God accomplished heavenly things so that His people might be of earthly use. When Christ ascended, He gave the Church "gifts" to help it achieve its assigned task, 4:7–13. These gifts are persons of the Word—apostles, prophets, evangelists, pastors and teachers. They are to proclaim to God's people what God has already done for them, to summon them to a life of unity within God's new community, and to equip them to use life as servants. (In 4:12, "ministry" means "service.")

**18** Chs. 4–6 give specific guidelines about what God's beloved children should do as they imitate their heavenly Father in all things, 5:1. Paul exhorts us to strive to lead a life worthy of the servant role to which we have been called, 4:1. He begs us to let Christ dwell in our hearts through faith, so that the roots of life might be anchored in His love for us, and that we might be empowered to offer loving service to those around us, 3:17. Life within the family circle is to be characterized by subjection to one another, 5:21. We are no longer to live as the unbelievers do, 4:17. We are to put off the old nature and the old way of life as one might discard undesirable clothing. We are to put on Christ's "character clothing" and reflect Him in all we think, say, and do. Our topics of conversation are to be different from those that tickle the ears of the dying world around us, 4:29, 5:12. We are to be on guard against the "empty words" of those who tempt us to compromise Christ's standards, 5:6. We are to demonstrate our heavenly citizenship in the family circle, in the immediate community, and in the world of business, labor, and politics.

**19** Samuel Taylor Coleridge was once moved to call Ephesians "one of the sublimest compositions of men." His evaluation is accurate!

56D

# Paul's Understanding of "Church" 56D

**1** Today, people speak of going to, or attending, church so that they might participate in religious activities in a facility. Paul would remind us that we are not called to *go* to church, but to *be* Jesus' church or community.

**2** The Greek word the New Testament translates as "church" is *ekklysia*—which literally means "those who have been called out." In the world of Paul's day, the *ekklysia* was the town council that met from time to time to deal with the affairs of the local community.

Note the **double-headed arrows** in the illustration.

- Its members *came together* to discuss and vote upon a variety of issues.
- They then *went forth* to carry out those decisions, or to see to it that they were implemented.

**3** **ILLUSTRATION 56D** depicts Paul's use of the term *ekklysia* in relation to faith and life within the Christian community.

    a. ***Symbol for God on Planet Earth:*** God made and owns Planet Earth.

    b. ***People in circles*** (*clockwise from lower right*)**:** God's praising people work at an endless variety of occupations: ***musicians***, ***engineers*** or ***mechanics***, ***farmers***, ***janitors***, ***chemists*** or ***pharmacists***. (The final circle is left empty so that people might write or sketch in whatever they do.)

    c. ***Arrows to and from the symbol for God:*** God calls people out from where they are and what they do into His presence to tell them who He is, what He has made and owns, and what He has done for their salvation (***Servant-King Jesus***, ***cross***, ***empty tomb***, ***rising arrow***). He then sends them back to do whatever they do in a manner that reflects the lifestyle of the Servant-King Jesus, and to praise and honor Him in all they think, say, and do (***raised hands***).

    d. If everyone were to ask only one question, "How can I use life at all times to reflect Jesus and serve others," what would this world be like? The answer is obvious and helps make clear what Paul has in mind when he speaks of God's goal to unite all things in Christ, Ephesians 1:9,10.

**4** God's people are, therefore, the *summoned* and the *sent*, the *called* and the *commissioned*, the *gathered* and the *scattered*. They gather in community to worship their Maker and Redeemer, and then go forth to reflect Jesus the Servant-Messiah in all that they think, say, and do.

56E

**1** Paul reminds us that we do not walk in uncontested territory. Satan is on the prowl, Ephesians 6:10–18. A fierce struggle rages in the universe between the powers of darkness and the authority of God. True, the outcome of the struggle has already been determined. Christ has conquered, and Christ is Lord. But Satan, the father of lies, remains on the battlefield and works to deceive people into thinking that he is still lord and that his values should prevail. Between the D-Day of Christ's resurrection and the V-Day of His return, Christians are involved in a mopping-up operation. They are to expose the enemy's lies, and to bring one foe after another into subjection to Christ—be that enemy an authority, a power, a dominion, or any other source of opposition, no matter what name might be applied to it, 1:21.

**2** **ILLUSTRATION 56E** depicts the nature of the enemy and the enemy's goals:

    a. Although there are similarities between **ILLUSTRATION 56D** and **ILLUSTRATION 56E**, God is not at the center of things. Satan is.

    b. The *five people in the surrounding circles* are not standing with hands raised in praise. Rather, they are standing in a *posture of indifference toward God*.

    c. The question uppermost in their minds is not: "How can I glorify God and reflect Jesus by serving others?" It is, "How can I benefit myself? What's in it for me?"

**3** C.S. Lewis wrote:

> *There is no neutral ground in the universe. Every square inch is claimed by God and counterclaimed by Satan.*

Lewis echoes accurately and vividly the teaching of Paul—and the entire New Testament.

There is reason to believe that the heresy Paul confronts in Colossians is a form of Gnosticism. (See Unit 51: 51A, *Gnosticism;* and 51B, *The Threat Posed by Gnosticism.*)

Many parallels exist between Ephesians and Colossians.

**1** While Paul was a prisoner in Rome, he was visited by Epaphras from Colossae, a city of Asia Minor about 125 miles (200 kilometers) east of Ephesus. Epaphras brought news about the progress being made in the Gentile church there; possibly he had oversight of it, Colossians 1:5–8. Although his report was positive and encouraging (1:6), he felt some anxiety. The church in Colossae was under threat. A "new teaching" was gaining a foothold and endangering the Gospel. Epaphras sought Paul's help to analyze and combat it.

**2** It is difficult to determine precisely what the heresy was. Paul does not define it, but confronts it with the Gospel. Indications are that the heresy involved the following:

    a. It attached importance to the powers of the spirit world. In referring to these, it used terms such as "thrones, dominions, rulers, powers," 1:16. Possibly it also involved angel worship, 2:18.

    b. The false teachers attached great importance to ritualistic observances in relation to feasts and fasts, food and drink, new moons and Sabbaths, and probably also circumcision, 2:11,16ff. They proclaimed their ideas as the true way of self-discipline and subjugation of the flesh, 2:20ff. An ascetic element was also involved: "Do not handle," "Do not taste," "Do not touch" (2:21), "a self-imposed piety, humility, and severe treatment of the body," 2:23.

    c. The false teachers declared that they possessed a higher, more profound occult knowledge derived from God, 2:8,18. When Paul uses terms such as knowledge, wisdom, understanding, and mystery, most likely he is using words that the heretics themselves used—but injecting into them their God-intended meaning.

**3** Paul answers these errors as follows:

    a. Christ is the Lord of the universe and of whatever powers exist within it. He is the creator of all things in heaven and on earth, and the conqueror of every evil force opposed to God and humanity, 1:15ff. All the "fullness" of the Godhead dwells in Him, 2:9. (Most likely the term "fullness" was one the false teachers used; Paul makes it serve his own purposes.) Those who exalt angels, emphasizing the functions of the good spiritual powers and the fear of the evil powers and authorities, are misguided. Christ is Lord of all; all things have been placed beneath His feet.

    b. The way to holiness and fellowship with God is not through asceticism or by self-centered efforts to control the passions; these practices lead to spiritual pride. The way to holiness is through putting on Christ and setting one's whole affection on Him, and by putting off all that is contrary to His will, 2:20ff; 3:11.

    c. Paul insists that it is vain to suggest that any earthly philosophy can be the true wisdom, 2:8. True wisdom is found only in that mystery, that "open secret" which is Christ. Christ dwells in all who receive Him and makes no distinction of persons, 1:27; 3:10ff.

**4** Paul saw that the Colossian heresy called into question the way of salvation in Christ. It obscured His unique greatness and denied the complete sufficiency of His atonement. It proclaimed and invoked other powers and practices as mediators between God and humanity. It was all the more dangerous because it claimed not to *supplant* but to *supplement* the Gospel of Christ. Paul's awareness of this led him to emphasize again and again that the Colossians were full and complete in the Gospel they had been taught, and that the treasures of divine wisdom are to be found in Christ alone, 2:2,3,9,10. The letter proclaims the Lordship of Christ—repeatedly, majestically, and triumphantly.

**1** While a prisoner in Rome, Paul was visited by Epaphras and Onesimus from Colossae. He was also visited by Epaphroditus from Philippi in Macedonia. Paul's work in Philippi is described in Acts 16:12–40; the church there was the first the apostle had established in Europe, and was predominantly Gentile.

**2** The Philippian church remained near and dear to Paul. Its members had treated Paul and his companions with consideration and generosity during their initial visit, and they continued to minister to Paul's needs after his departure. The apostle felt free to accept gifts from them and spoke of them as his partners in the Gospel, 1:5; 4:15. They contributed to his support on two occasions during his stay in Thessalonica (Philippians 4:16), and once while he was working in Corinth, 2 Corinthians 11:9. They also contributed generously to the offering taken up for the poor in Jerusalem, giving "beyond their means" even in the midst of a "severe ordeal of affliction" and while in the depths of poverty, 2 Corinthians 8:1–5.

**3** The church in Philippi felt moved to minister to Paul, even during his imprisonment. They gathered a gift for Paul and sent it to him by the hand of Epaphroditus. Furthermore, they instructed Epaphroditus to remain with Paul and help him as the need arose, Philippians 2:25. They showed this kind of consideration to Paul, despite the fact that they themselves were still being persecuted, 1:29. Epaphroditus helped Paul with such devotion that "he came close to death for the work of Christ, risking his life" to make up for those services the Philippians could not give to their apostle, 2:30.

**4** At the time of writing his letter to the Philippians, Paul is about to send Epaphroditus back to Philippi, 2:25–30. He sends with him a letter in which he brings his beloved Philippians up-to-date with news about himself, his trial, and the prospects for his release. He thanks them for their gift, and excuses and commends Epaphroditus, who, through no fault of his own, has not been able to carry out fully the desired ministry to Paul. Paul also comments, in a kindly and pastoral manner, about some of the issues that are troubling and dividing the congregation. He encourages them to stand firm in the faith despite persecution, and warns them to be on constant guard against threats being posed by Judaizers and libertine twisters of the Gospel.

**5** Philippians demonstrates in a touching manner Paul's attitude toward his sufferings. He is able to rejoice under the most trying circumstances, even when his very life is under threat. A note of joy rings throughout the letter. The secret of Paul's joy is his fellowship with Christ. He is secure in Him no matter what the future may hold. He encourages the Philippians to share his outlook. His letter says, "I rejoice!" and asks, "Do you?" Philippians contains a magnificent statement about the person of Jesus, 2:5–11. That passage alone is sufficient to make the letter a work of abiding worth. Paul's exhortations to the Philippians in 4:4–9 are sublime.

The New Testament has much to say about how Christians are to behave in their respective situations and callings. Some samples follow.

**1** In Ephesians, after appealing to believers to be subject to one another out of reverence for Christ (5:21), Paul offers directions to wives (5:22–24), husbands (5:25–33), children (6:1–3), parents (6:4), and slaves and masters, 6:5–9.

**2** In Colossians 3:18–4:1, Paul offers exhortations that parallel those given in Ephesians. Again, they are directed to wives, husbands, children, fathers, slaves, and masters.

**3** Similar exhortations are found in 1 Peter, where the writer offers advice concerning:

    a. The obedience to be given political authorities, 2:11–17.

    b. The attitude of a slave to a master, 2:18–25.

    c. How wives (3:1–6) and husbands (3:7) are to treat each other.

**4** The Gospel concerns itself with more than the cross. It concerns itself also with how people, who have stood at the foot of the cross and believed, behave after they return to their everyday situation in life. When the New Testament declares Jesus to be the Lord and King, it calls those who profess faith in Him to live in a manner that reflects His Servant-Kingship.

**5** **ILLUSTRATION 56H** reminds us that the Christian faith is not the *most important part of life*—it is *all of life*. The Christian walk is a full-time, sacred affair. Christians are to reflect Jesus, the Servant-King, in all they think, say, and do.

    a. *Government (**dome**):* Christians take an interest in, and serve in, government to enable all to live together harmoniously and happily at local, national, and international levels.

    b. *Study (**diplomas**):* Christians develop their minds and abilities to be equipped to serve others in a meaningful, helpful way.

    c. *Food and drink (**knife, fork, plate**):* Christians eat healthfully in order to live usefully. They eat to live; they do not live to eat.

    d. *Family life (**parents with children**):* The family is the basic unit of society. Parents influence children enormously, whether they realize it or not. The Christian faith must be taught, shared, modeled, and passed on in homes by parents who equip themselves to do so.

    e. *The use of money (**dollar sign**):* Money is service in a storable, transferable form. It is not wrong to have money. The question is: How did we get it, and how are we using it?

    f. *Sport and leisure activities (**ball**):* People need to exercise and participate in sporting activities and leisure pursuits to keep their bodies healthy and their minds alert.

    g. *Work (**factory**):* Christians see daily work as an opportunity to offer useful service or produce useful products.

    h. *Worship (**church facility**):* According to the Bible, church is always a community of people—never a building. Christians gather in an "ecclesiastical facility" to worship God together, to help each other grow in faith and discipleship, and to gather others into Jesus' kingdom.

**1** While Paul was in prison in Rome, he came into contact with at least two men from Colossae. The first was Epaphras, who was entrusted with the oversight of the church in Colossae. The second was a runaway slave called Onesimus. Onesimus had deserted his master, Philemon, and had helped himself to some of his master's goods prior to doing so. Obviously, Onesimus was badly named; his name means "useful." Onesimus headed for Rome, where eventually he came in to contact with Paul.

**2** Anyone who met Paul was bound to be introduced to Paul's friend, Jesus the Messiah. Onesimus met Him and came to faith in Him. Jesus transformed Onesimus with the result that he who had been *useless* became *useful*, v. 11. Although Paul would have been happy to retain Onesimus' services for himself, he knew that his master had first claim on him. Therefore, Paul sent him back to Philemon at Colossae.

**3** We read in the letter to the Colossians (4:9) that Onesimus made the journey with Tychicus, who delivered Paul's letter to the congregation in Colossae. Paul also sent a letter to Philemon with Onesimus. In it, he encouraged Philemon to receive his slave back in a kind and forgiving manner; at that time, captured runaway slaves were usually dealt with severely. Paul hints to Philemon that he would be happy to have Onesimus back in his own service, Philemon vv. 13,14.

**4** Although the letter is short, it reveals much about Paul's attitude toward solving problems within the social structures of the time. He did not openly advocate the abolition of slavery, but simply transformed the relationship between master and slave. He brought both Philemon and Onesimus into fellowship with Christ, thus bringing them into brotherly fellowship with one another. He suggested to Philemon that he should receive his now useful slave "back forever, no longer as a slave but more than a slave, a beloved brother," vv. 15,16.

**5** Paul did not set out to change *external structures* but *people's hearts* and *lives*. He saw the solution to the social ills of his time not in a *program* but in a *Person*. He knew that when the Person had transformed enough people, those transformed people would transform the external structures.

**56A** After Paul completed his third missionary journey, he visited Jerusalem. When a Jewish mob attacked him, the Romans placed him in protective custody and then took him to Caesarea where he was imprisoned. After spending two years behind bars, Paul (a Roman citizen) appealed to be tried by the Emperor. He was then taken to Rome and again imprisoned. During his time of incarceration, Paul wrote Ephesians, Philippians, Colossians, and Philemon—referred to as the Captivity Letters.

**56B** In the Captivity Letters, as in all his other writings, Paul bases his message on the pattern of the Sinai covenant, and Jesus' teachings about the nature of the New Covenant. The basic pattern of both formulations is "*Because I, God*, have done this for you, *therefore you, My children*, are to seek to walk My way at all times and in all places." Simply put, *Indicative—Imperative*.

**56C** In the first three chapters of *Ephesians* (most likely a circular letter), Paul defines who God is, and refers to the Person and work of Father, Son, and Holy Spirit. He then summons his readers to praise that Person. At the heart of these first three chapters is Paul's definition of God's plan for the universe and His will for the Church. God's children, Jesus' brothers and sisters, are to be a living display of God's original plan for humanity. Humanity at large is to be made aware of God's original plan by looking at the life of the Church. In the final three chapters of Ephesians, Paul offers specific guidelines concerning how God's people are to live as they strive to imitate their Servant Lord in the family circle, in the immediate community, and in the world of business, labor, and politics.

**56D** In dealing with these issues, Paul reminds God's people of all ages that they are not called merely to *go to Church*; they are to *be God's Church*. In dealing with this issue, Paul makes use of the Greek term *ekklysia*—a term that implies being both *summoned* and *sent*. God's people gather in community to worship and praise their Maker and Redeemer, and then go forth to reflect their Servant Lord, Jesus the Messiah, in all they think, say, and do.

**56E** Paul reminds God's people that they do not walk in uncontested territory. Satan is constantly on the prowl seeking to mislead God's people and to seduce them to *live for self*, rather than *for God and others*. Even though Jesus conquered Satan at the cross, God's people are to devote life to carrying out a mopping-up operation by exposing Satan's lies and by devoting life to bringing all spiritual foes into subjection to Jesus, the Servant Messiah, as Lord.

**56F** There are many similarities between the contents of Ephesians and *Colossians*. Colossians was written to counter a threat posed by false teachers who attached considerable importance to ritualistic observances, and to the powers of the spirit world and their brand of "knowledge." These false teachers obscured Christ's greatness and denied the sufficiency of His atonement. Paul countered the threat with profound truths about the preeminence of Christ.

**56G** Paul wrote *Philippians* to thank a congregation that was dear to him for their continuing interest in his welfare. He also encouraged them to continue to walk in the paths of Him who, although He was God, humbled Himself and became obedient unto death—even to the point of surrendering to death on the cross. The first eleven verses of chapter two contain some of Paul's most profound insights in relation to Jesus' Person, saving work, and exaltation.

**56H** In all his letters, including the Captivity Letters, Paul offers numerous insights concerning how, out of reverence to Christ, God's people are to behave in their respective situations and callings: wives, husbands, children, parents, slaves, and masters.

**56I** *Philemon* was addressed to the owner of the runaway slave, Onesimus, who had come to faith through his association with Paul. Paul encourages Philemon to receive his former "useless" slave back as a "useful" brother in Christ. Nowhere in his writings does Paul advocate the abolition of slavery. Rather, he suggested a transformation in the relationship between master and slave; both are to see themselves as brothers of Christ, and brothers of each other.

# CROSS WAYS

**6 SECTION**

**UNITS 51–60**

# The Letters and Revelation

# UNIT 57

## 1 and 2 Timothy; Titus

*Paul's Counsel to Pastors*

57A

**1** The Pastoral Letters are addressed to *Timothy and Titus*. Paul left Timothy in charge of the church in *Ephesus*, and Titus in charge of the church on the island of *Crete*. First and Second Timothy and Titus are today referred to as "the Pastoral Letters." They have not always been called that.

    a. The Muratorian Canon (the earliest list of New Testament books, A.D. 170) classified them as personal letters, distinguishing them from Paul's other letters written to churches and communities.

    b. Thomas Aquinas (about A.D. 1250) said that 1 Timothy was "a kind of pastoral rule," providing Timothy with everything necessary "for the training of bishops." Hence, by the seventeenth century, they were referred to as the Pontifical letters.

    c. In A.D. 1726–27, Paul Anton gave a series of lectures at Halle, during which he referred to these three writings as "the supreme example of writings suitable to those who seek preparation for, and guidance in, the Christian ministry." The title, the Pastoral Letters, has been applied to them ever since. This defines their purpose, for they were written that "you may know how one ought to behave in the household of God, which is the church of the living God," 1 Timothy 3:15.

**2** Although **ILLUSTRATION 57A** introduces the New Testament concept of "pastor," some of its details reflect 21st-century practices rather than those of the first century. (The early apostles did not wear clerical collars, and, although women served in various roles in the early church, few—if any—were ordained as pastors.) The illustration makes the following points:

    a. When Jesus completed His work on earth, He "ascended into heaven," Acts 1:9. In doing so, Jesus did not *withdraw* His presence, but *transformed* it. (The *upper section* of the illustration shows the **glorified Jesus "ascending."**)

    b. When Jesus ascended, He gave parting *gifts* to His people. These gifts were, and still are, persons of the Word: "apostles, prophets, evangelists, pastors and teachers," Ephesians 4:8,11. (In **ILLUSTRATION 57A**, the parting gifts are depicted as **clergy, superimposed on gift boxes, complete with an open Bible.**)

    c. These persons of the Word have a servant role (**servant figures on Bibles**)—to study, teach, and proclaim Jesus' Word. They are not to do the work of the Church for other people, but to equip other people to be the Church. According to Ephesians 4:12, their task is to:

       ● *equip the saints for the work of ministry.* (RSV, NRSV)

       ● *equip God's people for work in God's service.* (NEB)

       ● *prepare all God's people for the work of Christian service.* (TEV)

**3** Persons of the Word are not called to serve *people's whims*, but *Jesus' will*. They are to serve people, not as *they* might want to be served, but as *Jesus* wants them to be served. Jesus writes the agenda; people do not.

**1** It is difficult to reconstruct the details of Paul's life after his release from his first imprisonment in Rome. Because Acts offers no help on the subject, one must guess at the history of this period from comments in the Pastoral Letters themselves. They contain limited information. The sequence of events, therefore, remains somewhat obscure.

**2** It seems reasonably certain that Paul was released at the end of the two years' imprisonment referred to in Acts 28:30; there is no evidence that this period of detention ended in martyrdom. Although Paul had, prior to this imprisonment, expressed a desire to visit Spain (Romans 15:28), the Pastoral Letters make no reference to that proposed venture having taken place. However, the Pastoral Letters do indicate that he achieved his other hope—to revisit his former fields of labor in Asia and Macedonia, Philemon 22; Philippians 2:24.

**3** It seems reasonable to suggest that Paul returned to the east by way of Crete, leaving Titus there to continue the work he himself had begun, Titus 1:5. Paul possibly visited Ephesus for a short time and gave Timothy the oversight of the church in that large and important city. From Ephesus, Paul continued on to Macedonia and wrote to Timothy from there. The instructions he gave Timothy indicate that much work needed to be done in Ephesus, 1 Timothy 1:3. He wrote the letter to Titus either from Macedonia or while on the way to Nicopolis where he planned to spend the winter. Titus was to join Paul in Nicopolis after Artemas or Tychicus had relieved him in Crete, Titus 3:12. Paul eventually visited Troas, Corinth, and Miletus, after which he wrote 2 Timothy; see 2 Timothy 4:13,20. He was then arrested—where is uncertain—and imprisoned in Rome. This imprisonment was much more serious, and Paul saw no hope of release. He summoned Timothy (his "beloved child," 2 Timothy 1:2) to visit him before the end came. Paul's martyrdom took place during the reign of Nero, but not during the great persecution of A.D. 64. Paul would not have asked Timothy to come to him while that particular persecution was in progress, nor would he have lamented that none of the Roman Christians stood by him during his "first defense" (2 Timothy 4:16) if they themselves were faced with the threat of death because of their faith. The writing of 2 Timothy must, therefore, be dated before A.D. 63, or as late as A.D. 67.

**4** Acts and the Pauline Letters mention Timothy frequently. His father was Greek and his mother a Jewess. He was already a Christian when Paul visited Lystra during his second missionary journey, Acts 16:1. At that time, Timothy joined Paul's company and remained one of his most faithful companions and fellow workers. On occasion, Paul sent him on difficult missions. He was with Paul during the period of the apostle's house arrest in Rome, Colossians 1:1, Philippians 1:1. When Paul left him in Ephesus (1 Timothy 1:3), he was still relatively young, 1 Timothy 4:12.

**5** Although Acts does not mention Titus, Paul's letters do. Titus 1:4 suggests that he was converted by Paul himself ("my loyal child in the faith"). He was Greek, Galatians 2:3. During his third missionary journey, Paul sent Titus on a difficult mission to Corinth, and after his return Paul sent him back to help the Corinthian congregation gather the offering for the poor at Jerusalem. After Paul's release from his first Roman imprisonment, he placed Titus in charge of the church on Crete, Titus 1:5. The last information we have about Titus is that he went to Dalmatia, most likely to carry out mission work, 2 Timothy 4:10.

**6** The term "Pastoral" can be more appropriately applied to 1 Timothy and Titus than to 2 Timothy. Although 2 Timothy contains pastoral elements, it is basically a personal letter in a class by itself; 1 Timothy and Titus are much more official in tone and were addressed, not only to Timothy and Titus, but also to the churches these men cared for. The concluding greeting in each one is, "Grace be with you" ("you" is plural in form); Titus 3:15 adds the word "all."

**7** All three Letters were apparently written within a short period of time. Their common purpose is to equip Timothy and Titus for present and future responsibilities. Although they contain considerable instruction about ecclesiastical administration, it would be wrong to assume that the underlying purpose of each was merely to supply information and instruction.

**8** Paul's reasons for writing 2 Timothy are more obvious than his reasons for writing the other Pastoral Letters. He delivers final admonitions and exhortations to his (at times) timid successor to act worthily in his high calling, 1:6,8,13ff; 2:1,22; 3:14; 4:1ff. Paul longs to see him and twice urges him to come to him soon (4:9,21), although he is not sure that this will be possible, 4:6. Paul warns Timothy about ungodly men who trouble the Christian community—and exhorts him to avoid them. He is to entrust the traditions to worthy men capable of passing those traditions on to others, 2:2.

**9** The purposes behind 1 Timothy and Titus are not so immediately apparent. Paul had only recently left them. No doubt, much of what the Letters contain had already been discussed in personal conversation. One might wonder why Paul considered it necessary to set forth such detailed information about qualifications for office bearers in the church, unless the letters were intended to strengthen the hands of Paul's representatives in their respective areas.

**10** Paul felt no need to write *theological* treatises to friends who had heard him speak about the great Christian doctrines on many occasions. The Pastoral Letters are basically *practical* in their concern. They refer to many functions and activities within the church. Paul urges his friends:

- to adhere faithfully to the true faith;
- to defend the faith against heretical teachings;
- to appoint qualified officials in the local churches;
- to regulate public worship, and
- to exhort the faithful to lead exemplary lives in keeping with their positions and responsibilities.

## THE ISSUE

A careful reading of the Pastorals reveals that there is more at stake than the competence of Timothy and Titus. Concern about the threat of false teaching occupies a central place in both works. (The false teaching described bears all the marks of first-century Gnosticism; see Unit 51.) There is a desire throughout to expose and attack false teaching. There are hints that some holding influential positions in the Church are succumbing to it—hence the concern throughout the Pastorals about qualifications for office and discrimination in ordaining. The church was being upset by:

**1** Insubordinate persons, empty talkers, and Judaizing deceivers who upset whole families and taught their heresies merely to make money, 1 Timothy 6:3–5; Titus 3:9,10. Although they claimed to be teachers of the Law, they did not understand its true meaning and what role it should play in the life of Christians, 1 Timothy 1:6–11. They even dared to place themselves above the Law.

**2** Those who played around with "myths and endless genealogies" (1 Timothy 1:4), "profane myths and old wive's tales" (4:7), and "Jewish myths," Titus 1:14.

**3** Those who taught that matter is evil, marriage is to be renounced, and certain foods are not to be eaten, 1 Timothy 4:1–5.

**4** Those who taught that the resurrection was already past, 2 Timothy 2:18.

## THE RESPONSE

**1** The Pastorals deal with the combination of heresy and immorality by demanding that orthodox belief and God-pleasing behavior be upheld. Numerous terms are used in the appeals for orthodoxy—terms that denote that the Christian faith is by now a systematized body of doctrine: "the faith," 1 Timothy 1:19; "the truth," 1 Timothy 3:15; "knowledge of truth," 1 Timothy 2:4; "your teaching," 1 Timothy 4:16; "the commandment," 1 Timothy 6:14; "the standard of sound teaching," 2 Timothy 1:13. Paul lashes out at those who peddle false doctrines, declaring that they have corrupt minds, Titus 1:15,16. A heretic is to be admonished once or twice, but after that, no one is to have anything to do with him, Titus 3:10.

**2** Conversely, there are also those who are "an ornament to the doctrine of God our Savior," Titus 2:10. They are responsible stewards of what has been entrusted to them—even as Paul has entrusted to Timothy the Gospel that God first entrusted to him, 1 Timothy 1:11, 6:20. Timothy is to guard that trust and pass it on to other responsible persons, 2 Timothy 2:2. God will take good care of His truth until Judgment Day, 2 Timothy 1:12.

**3** True religion begins with baptism (Titus 3:5), and is fostered by Christian upbringing, 2 Timothy 3:15. (Timothy is a third-generation Christian, 2 Timothy 1:5.) The Scriptures play a key role in nurture; they are to be read publicly and used in the family circle, 1 Timothy 4:13; 2 Timothy 3:15.

**4** Church leaders can expect suffering (2 Timothy 1:11,12) and conflict, 1 Timothy 1:18. Timothy must fight the good fight of faith and endure suffering to achieve self-discipline, 1 Timothy 6:12. He must remember the price soldiers, farmers, and athletes pay to achieve their goals, 2 Timothy 2:1–7. There will be persecution from civil authorities; Paul is no stranger to this, 2 Timothy 3:10–12. One must endure such difficulties with patience, secure in the knowledge that God cares for His own and will reward the faithful on Judgment Day, 2 Timothy 4:8. At the same time, Timothy is to avoid conflict, strive for peace, and live in conformity to the law, 2 Timothy 2:22; 1 Timothy 1:8–11.

**5** What constitutes God-pleasing behavior? Believers are to demonstrate their allegiance to Christ through responsible citizenship, within both their own fellowship and the wider community, 1 Timothy 3:15. They must be models of good deeds and self-control, renounce false beliefs and

practices, and live sober and upright lives, Titus 2:6,7,12; 3:1,2. Slaves are to obey their masters "so that the name of God and the teaching may not be blasphemed," 1 Timothy 6:1.

**6** Believers are not to fall victim to the ascetic notions that some false teachers were advocating, such as abstinence from marriage, and from certain foods and wine, 1 Timothy 4:1–5; 5:23. All these things come from God, and are to be accepted gratefully and used with thankfulness. Although exercise has some merit, it does not help achieve true spirituality, 1 Timothy 4:7,8.

**7** Solemn warnings are directed against coveting money and material goods, 1 Timothy 6:6–10, 17–19. Those who covet these things expose themselves to numerous dangers and jeopardize their salvation.

## Leaders and Liturgy

### BISHOPS/ELDERS, DEACONS

**1** The Pastorals define the qualifications of bishops/elders (1 Timothy 3:1–7) and deacons (3:8–13), and list factors to consider in appointing bishops/elders, Titus 1:5–9. Advice about ecclesiastical conduct given to Timothy (1 Timothy 4:6–16; 6:11–16; 2 Timothy 1:8–14; 2:1–7,14–26) and Titus (3:8–11) speaks to future incumbents as well.

**2** Appointees are to be righteous, clean-living persons, able and courteous teachers, equipped to state their case and support it—those who have proved themselves over a period of time. They must be able to rule their own family wisely and well. If they are incapable of ruling their own family, the chances are that they are incapable of ruling in the church. They are to be held in high regard within and outside the church. The early church did not base its hope of success on *new systems*; it based it on *new persons* who were in a vital relationship with Jesus the Messiah, 1 Timothy 3:1–7.

**3** A bishop/elder is to be selected by a deliberate process and commissioned by a ceremony involving the laying on of hands, 1 Timothy 4:14; 2 Timothy 1:6. Those so appointed are to receive financial aid from the churches, 1 Timothy 5:17,18. Complaints against a bishop/elder are to be handled carefully, 1 Timothy 5:19.

**4** Women are to avoid ostentatious adornment and not to usurp teaching authority over men, 1 Timothy 2:9–15. Provision is to be made for the care of widows deserving of the church's support, 1 Timothy 5:3–16.

### CREEDS AND HYMNS

**1** The Pastorals contain what appear to be fragments of early Christian hymns (1 Timothy 3:16; 2 Timothy 2:11–13) and a fragment of an early creed, 2 Timothy 2:8.

**2** The Pastorals repeatedly stress the importance of holding to "the true faith" in sincerity. They specify numerous details of this true faith. All created things are good, 1 Timothy 4:4. Salvation has already appeared, Titus 2:11. The work of redemption is done, 1 Timothy 3:16. Believers look forward to a Kingdom in heaven, 2 Timothy 4:18.

**3** Christ's future role is that of Judge, 2 Timothy 4:1,8. Although eternal life was promised long ago, it has now been manifested through the preaching of Paul and the successors to whom he entrusted his ministry. The title "Savior" is ascribed to God (1 Timothy 2:3; 4:10; Titus 2:10; 3:4) and Christ, Titus 1:4; 3:6; see also 1 Timothy 1:2 and 2:5.

**1** On occasion, one hears it said, "Money is the root of all evil." The Bible does not say that. Paul writes in 1 Timothy 6:6–10:

> *Of course, there is great gain in godliness combined with contentment; for we brought nothing into this world, so that we can take nothing out of it; but if we have food and clothing, we will be content with these. But those who want to be rich fall into temptation and are trapped by many senseless and harmful desires that plunge them into ruin and destruction. For the love of money is the root of all kinds of evil, and in their eagerness to be rich some have wandered away from the faith and pierced themselves with many pains.*

Hence, the *love of money*, not *money itself*, is the root of all evil. Money in itself is a lifeless, morally neutral thing—neither good nor bad.

**2** In warning against the love of money, Paul reflects a warning that Jesus made repeatedly during His earthly ministry, Luke 6:20–26, Blessings and Woes; 12:13–21, the parable of the Rich Fool; 14:25–33, the Cost of Discipleship; 16:1–13, the parable of the Dishonest Manager; 16:19–31, the parable of the Rich Man and Lazarus; 18:18–25, the parable of the Rich Ruler.

**3** Money can be thought of as merely Christian effort, love, and service in a storable, exchangeable form. Money is self in storage, stored servanthood, that can be put to work quickly by signing a check or handing over banknotes. We can use it to empower others to serve in situations where we cannot be present personally; note Luke 10:25–37, vv. 34,35 in particular.

**4** Unfortunately, many people assume they "own" their possessions, and when asked to contribute to a Christian cause, they feel that they themselves must decide what they will *give* of what is *theirs* (**ILLUSTRATION 57E**, *left section*). They assume that, after they have given their "fair share" to God, the rest is theirs to do with as they please. However, the Bible would have us view things differently (**ILLUSTRATION 57E**, *right section*).

    a. We own nothing. God made and owns everything, including the body in which we reside, Exodus 19:5; 1 Corinthians 4:7. We give God nothing; we merely use what is God's.

    b. The question that Christians must ask is, "How much of what belongs to God should I use for my own needs?"

    c. We do not own God's creation. We merely manage it. God's people are to practice Christian *management and distribution*, rather than Christian *giving*. After all, we cannot *give* what belongs to another.

    d. The principle set forth in 4c above applies to all of life—not just to life in the organized church. The kingdom of God embraces all of life. The traditional spiritual-secular distinction is invalid. There is no such thing as a secular realm.

**5** The understanding of God's people in relation to Christian *management* would be helped if the First Article of the Apostles' Creed were amended to read:

> *I believe in God the Father Almighty, Maker **and Owner** of Heaven and Earth.*

57F

# All Things under Jesus' Feet

**1** Unit 57 brings to a close the survey of Paul's writings. Although **ILLUSTRATION 57F** is not based on a passage from the Pastoral Letters, it serves a useful purpose in summing up the burning conviction that Paul reflects in all his letters—and the truth that all preachers and teachers of God's Word must proclaim with their lips and lives. In Ephesians 1:22, the apostle writes, "And He (God) has put all things under His (Jesus') feet."

**2** Ancient practices lie behind Paul's statement. In the ancient Near East, a king had the faces or figures of conquered enemies carved or embroidered on to his footstool, and then placed his feet upon it. The implications were obvious; the king had authority over those whose images appeared on the footstool.

**3** In **ILLUSTRATION 57F**, *Jesus' feet* rest on a *footstool*. The *crowned figures* on Jesus' feet point to His role as King of the universe. Reading *clockwise* from the *top left corner* of the footstool, the six symbols are:

    a. *The power of sin (**symbol for sin**):* Throughout His life, Jesus submitted to the will of His Father—not to the power of sin. In so doing, Jesus broke sin's hold on the human race. Jesus is sin's master. Jesus declares our sins forgiven. See Romans 6:5–11.

    b. *The law (**law tablets**):* Jesus, the God-man, was perfectly obedient to His Father's will for humanity. In Colossians 2:13–15 (note v. 15 in particular), Paul uses the picture of a military commander, returning in triumphant procession after conquering his foes, to depict Jesus' conquering of the Law. Jesus alone may declare God's disposition toward sinners. Jesus alone may declare what God requires of humanity.

    c. *Judgment and condemnation (**gavel**):* Jesus' victory over the law destroyed its authority to judge and condemn those who put their trust in Him, Romans 8:1,2,33,34.

    d. *Satan (**demonic face**):* Jesus' ministry was a battle with Satan and his realm. Jesus won the battle, Romans 16:20; 1 John 3:8. Although Satan can trouble and tempt God's people, Satan does not have the last word. Jesus does!

    e. *The heavenly powers (**crown with astrological symbols**):* Here the reference is to terms Paul uses in Ephesians 1:21 (*rule, authority, power, dominion*), 6:12 (*rulers, authorities, cosmic powers, spiritual forces of evil in the heavenly places*); Colossians 1:16 (*thrones, dominions, rulers, powers*); see also Romans 8:38,39. Jesus has authority over every so-called power in the universe.

    f. *Death (**tombstone and skull**):* Jesus is Lord over death and the grave. The grave must obey when Jesus commands it to yield up its victims, 1 Corinthians 15:50–57.

**4** Paul vividly sums up Jesus' Lordship when he writes:

*Therefore God also highly exalted Him, and gave Him the name that is above every name, so that at the name of Jesus every knee should bend, in heaven and on earth and under the earth, and every tongue confess that Jesus Christ is Lord, to the glory of God the Father.* (Philippians 2:9–11)

# Who Wrote the Pastorals?

 The early Church attributed the Pastorals to Paul. However, since the beginning of the nineteenth century, many have questioned this. Some scholars suggest the following:

   a.  The errors attacked in the Pastorals are Gnostic errors of the second century A.D.

   b.  The Pastorals reflect a second-century stage of Church organization.

   c.  Their style, tone, and vocabulary lack a Pauline character. Elsewhere, Paul fights for the truth with the skill of a fencer. He presents the truth about Jesus the Messiah in a manner that enables false positions to be seen in their true light. The Pastorals lack Paul's usual rugged fervor and fire. They hope that a well-ordered church will stem the tide of heresy. Possibly, a later writer made use of Pauline fragments to produce a work in Paul's name that would possess the necessary authority to counter threats to the church of his day— possibly in the early second century.

Other scholars respond to the opinions expressed in point 1 above as follows:

   a.  The heresy that the Pastoral Letters attack is not a second-century Gnosticism, but a form of Jewish Gnosticism known from sources other than Paul.

   b.  The ecclesiastical organization reflected in the Pastorals fits in with that of the mid-first century, as known from other sources. Ignatius of Antioch (martyred about A.D. 117) refers to a much more developed ecclesiastical system in his works.

   c.  Although the language of the Pastorals is different from that found in Paul's other writings, much of it is unique because it speaks to special situations. Paul's mind was brilliant and flexible enough to address different situations with appropriate terminology. Or perhaps Paul produced the ideas and some other person did the actual writing in a style different from Paul's usual style.

The debate continues. What finally matters is not who *held* the pen, but who *inspired* the pen.
The Holy Spirit has given the Pastorals to the Church. It is more edifying to listen to their *message* than to debate their *origins*.

**57A** When Jesus ascended into heaven, He did not *withdraw* His presence; He *transformed* it. The ascended, transformed Jesus gave, and continues to give, gifts to His people. These gifts are persons of His Word: apostles, prophets, evangelists, and pastors and teachers. Apostles are those "sent forth." Prophets are those who "speak forth." Evangelists are those who "witness to win" others for Christ. The terms "pastors and teachers" denote those who are to shepherd and teach God's flock. None who fulfill these functions dare do so to have people notice them. Their one desire is that they empower others to notice, believe in, and follow Jesus, the Good Shepherd.

**57B** It is difficult to determine the details of Paul's travels and ministry after he was finally released from prison in Rome. Although, in the Captivity Letters, Paul expresses a desire to visit Spain, the Pastoral Letters make no reference to such a journey. There is reason to believe that Paul was eventually imprisoned a second time in Rome—and martyred.

Acts and Paul's other letters make frequent reference to Timothy who accompanied Paul on his second and third missionary journeys. Although Acts makes no reference to Titus, Paul's letters do. After his release from prison in Rome, Paul placed Timothy in charge of the work in Ephesus and put Titus in charge of the work on the island of Crete.

**57C** Concern about the threat of false teaching plays an important role in the Pastoral Letters. The church was being upset by insubordinate persons, empty talkers, and Judaizing deceivers who taught their heresies merely to make money—and they upset whole families in the process. They set themselves above the teachings of the Jewish Law and did not understand the role that it should play in the life of God's people. There is reason to believe that the false teachers were embracing both Gnostic and Jewish beliefs in that they taught that matter is evil, marriage is to be renounced, and certain foods are not to be eaten.

In the Pastoral Letters, Paul instructs God's people to adhere firmly to the true faith, to defend it against heretical teachings, to appoint qualified officials in their churches, to regulate public worship, and to exhort the faithful to lead exemplary lives in accordance with the duties they are to carry out whatever position they hold in life.

**57D** The Pastoral Letters address the issue of the qualifications of bishops/elders and deacons, and factors to be borne in mind when appointing them. Among other things, bishops/elders must be able to rule their own family wisely and well; if they cannot do that, most likely they will lack the ability to direct the Church in a God-pleasing manner.

The Pastoral Letters contain fragments of early Christian hymns and creeds. They stress the importance of holding to "the true faith" in sincerity.

**57E** In his first letter to Timothy, Paul refers to the love of money being the root of all evil (6:10). Money is not itself evil. However, people can handle it in an evil manner. It is important that God's people understand that God made and owns everything, that we mere mortals own nothing, and that in all things we are merely managers of Another's property. Within the Christian community, the goal is not to encourage people to *give more* but to inspire them to *rob less*.

**57F** In his letter to the Ephesians, Paul speaks of God "putting all things under Jesus' feet." While Paul does not refer specifically to this concept in his letters to Timothy and Titus, the thought sums up the conviction that Paul reflects in all his letters.

**57G** Although the early Church attributed the writing of the Pastoral Letters to Paul himself, down through the centuries many have questioned this belief. However, what matters is not who *held* the pen but who *inspired* the pen. It is more edifying to listen to the message of the Pastoral Letters than to debate their authorship and origins.

# CROSS WAYS®

## 6 SECTION

### UNITS 51–60
## The Letters and Revelation

## UNIT 58
### Hebrews

*The Superiority of Christ*

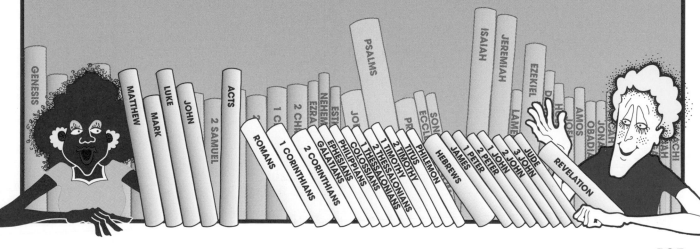

**1** ***Tabernacle canceled out*** (*lower left*)**:** The worship rituals practiced before Jesus' coming were but imperfect shadows of His final, perfect work.

**2** ***Jesus the Messiah*** is now the link between God and humanity, between the heavenly and earthly realms.

**3** ***Rent veil leading to God's presence*** (*torn white line down center*)**:** Jesus does not minister in a transient, earthly sanctuary, but in the perfect, eternal, Heavenly Sanctuary.

**4** ***Priest's hat*** (*center*)**:** Hebrews sets forth the superiority of Jesus the Messiah's Person and speaks of His work as the ultimate, once-and-for-all Priest.

**5** ***Crown*** (*center left*)**:** Because Jesus is God's Son and the King of the Universe, God's people are to strive to live as members of His eternal people.

**6** ***View across the Ancient Near East*** (*lower section*)**:** Jesus' saving work avails for all humanity—not merely for physical descendants of Abraham. Through Jesus' perfect sacrifice, those who belong to Him have access to the very presence of God.

## DESTINATION

**1** The letter's opening sentences contain no information about its recipients or where they lived. The traditional title, "To the Hebrews," was not part of the original letter. Scholars suggest that it was added during the second century A.D.

**2** Some suggest that the letter was written to a group of Jews and Gentiles who had embraced the Christian faith. Others suggest that it was sent to a group of Jews who had broken with orthodox Judaism, but were not convinced that Jesus was the Messiah. Still others think that it was addressed to Gentile Christians in danger of lapsing into unbelief.

**3** Because the writer goes to considerable lengths to demonstrate that the New Testament revelation is superior to that of the Old Testament, the most plausible suggestion is that it was written to Jewish Christians in danger of reverting to Judaism. Furthermore, chs. 6 and 10 contain a series of warnings that to fall away from faith in Jesus the Messiah is to crucify the Son of God anew (6:6) and to profane the blood of the covenant, 10:29. The author wrote to those who had tasted the goodness of the Lord to discourage them from reverting to their former faith, 6:4–6.

**4** It is uncertain where the recipients lived. The letter contains a greeting from "those from Italy" (13:24), possibly people with the author who were sending greetings to their home church in Italy. Some suggest that the recipients were members of one of the house churches Paul refers to in Romans 16:5,14,15. (The letter was first quoted by *Roman* writers, Clement of Rome and Hermas.)

**5** The message reflects a personal relationship between the author and his readers. He had lived among them and knew them well. Although he was not among them at the time of writing, he hoped to return to them soon, 13:19,23.

## AUTHOR

**1** The author's identity remains unknown. With the exception of 1 John, Hebrews is the only New Testament letter to omit an opening greeting that mentions the writer's name. About A.D. 215, Clement of Alexandria suggested that Paul wrote it in Hebrew for Jews and that Luke translated it into Greek. About A.D. 250, Origen of Alexandria delivered his famous verdict, "Only God knows for certain who wrote Hebrews." Tertullian ascribed it to Barnabas. By the end of the fourth century, the western Church had accepted it as Pauline and canonical.

**2** The reasons for denying Pauline authorship are of sufficient weight to be compelling. A more recent guess is that Priscilla and Aquila wrote it. Luther suggested it came from Apollos' pen. Most likely, Origen's opinion remains valid. Although we do not know whose hand held the pen, we believe that the Holy Spirit guided it.

## PURPOSE

**1** Some scholars suggest that Hebrews was addressed to Jewish Christians in danger of relapsing to Judaism, 3:12; 13:9–14. They had previously shown true faith and sincere love, 6:10. When facing persecution, they had helped each other deal with the challenge, 10:32–34.

**2** However, although they had demonstrated courage in crisis, they were growing faint in their struggle with sin, 12:4,12. Possibly, they were being ridiculed by fellow Jews who pointed to the weakness of Christ in that He finished up on a cross. They were static in their faith and were neglecting the strengthening experience of public worship, 5:11–14; 10:25. No doubt their former faith retained an attraction for them—with its revered institutions, its imposing focal point (the Jerusalem Temple), its solemn rituals, and the security it enjoyed under the Roman Law as a *religio licita* (a *permitted religion*).

**3** To counter this temptation, the author speaks a "word of exhortation," 13:22. He urges his readers to "hold fast to the confession of our hope without wavering," 10:23. He encourages them to look "to Jesus the pioneer and perfecter of our faith, who for the sake of the joy that was set before Him endured the cross, disregarding its shame," 12:2. Jesus will empower them to overcome their spiritual weariness and faintheartedness, 12:3.

## DATE

**1** Only limited information is available for dating the letter. Timothy was still alive, 13:23. The recipients were brought to faith by those who, some time previously, had been personal disciples of the Lord, 2:3. Some date Hebrews prior to A.D. 64, just before Nero's persecution. Others suggest a date shortly before A.D. 70, and still others opt for a date as late as A.D. 80–90. Clement of Rome referred to it in A.D. 96—indicating that it must have been produced before that time.

**2** The writer devotes considerable space to pointing out that the old system of priesthood and sacrifices had been superseded by a greater and more perfect priesthood and sacrifice. It would have been strange for him not to mention the destruction of Jerusalem and the Temple if that event had already taken place—which suggests a date shortly before A.D. 70. However, it can be argued that the writer is concerned with the rituals themselves—not the building in which they were carried out (he refers to the ancient Tabernacle rather than to the Temple).

## CENTRAL THEME

**1** The central theme of Hebrews is the true worship of God through the authentic High Priest—Jesus. The Jewish sacrificial system is obsolete. It has been superseded. The former sanctuary on earth was but a shadow of the perfect sanctuary in heaven. Through Jesus, God has opened up a way for His people to attain access to His presence in the heavenly sanctuary. The members of the new covenant community are the true heirs of the biblical tradition, 8:6–13.

**2** Although Hebrews gives the impression of being a theological treatise, it is basically a pastoral letter concerned with the salvation of its readers. Whoever wrote it was aware that he had to give an account of his leadership, 13:17.

# Contents

Hebrews reads like a sermon. Sections that instruct are followed by sections that admonish and exhort. The work makes use of more than a hundred quotations from, or allusions to, the Old Testament—in particular, Psalms 2,8,110 and Jeremiah 31. Chapters 11–13 draw heavily on the history of Israel.

The basic concern of Hebrews is the superiority of Jesus the Messiah. After a stately prologue (1:1–4), the writer focuses on the superiority of Jesus' Person (1:5–4:13) and work, 4:14–10:18. The third section of the letter contains exhortations and admonitions (10:19–13:19), and a benediction, 13:20–25.

## PROLOGUE
### Hebrews 1:1-4

God revealed Himself in former times through the prophets. But now the Messianic Age has come and, with it, the end time—the final period of religious history. Now God's own Son, the Creator and Goal of all things, is God's means of communicating divine truth to humanity. The Son is the perfect representation of the Father's being. He took part in the initial creative process and continues to sustain what He created. He entered the human realm to destroy the power of sin. After completing what He came to do, He returned (through His resurrection and ascension) to the presence of the Father. He is unique. No person or creature can match His dignity. He is now enthroned in splendor.

## THE SUPERIORITY OF JESUS' PERSON
### Hebrews 1:5-4:13

**1** **1:5–14:** In ch. 1, the writer quotes a number of Psalms that speak of Jesus' divine kingship and role in creation. He also states that Jesus is superior to the angels. Why this comparison? Judaism said that angels had been involved in the giving of the Law at *Sinai* as ministering *servants*, and they continue to *serve* those who share in the salvation that *Jesus* accomplished.

**2** **2:1–4:** Jesus' absolute supremacy should serve to strengthen Christians in their desire to remain faithful to their Lord. If violations of the old Mosaic covenant (mediated through *angels*) were treated severely, how much more should one seek not to fall from the covenant established through the *greater Son*. The message and mission of Jesus is proclaimed by divinely-appointed witnesses, and confirmed by divine power through signs and miracles.

**3** **2:5–18:** Yes, Jesus had to suffer—but that experience did not call into question His unique greatness. Although Jesus lived a truly human life during His time on earth, He now shares fully in the honor and glory of His Father. It was only to be expected that His Father would have required Jesus to walk the path of humiliation and suffering. This was an essential part of Jesus' work as priest. Through Jesus, God has brought many into membership in His family. It is fitting, then, that the Father should have made His instrument to accomplish that (namely, Jesus) perfect through suffering. In so doing, Jesus identified with those He came to save. He identified Himself with Abraham's descendants, and experienced all that they did, in order to function as High Priest and to make atonement for their sins.

**4** **3:1–6:** Jesus is superior to Moses. Although Moses mediated the Law and was faithful to God, he nevertheless was faithful *within* the house of God—he was himself a member of God's chosen people. Jesus is much more than that. He is *over* God's house. Moses was God's *servant*; his role was that of law-giver. Jesus is God's *Son*; His role is to be God's law and will in human form. Jesus can lead us, not just into geographical Canaan, but into Eternal Rest in the Heavenly Canaan.

**5** **3:7–4:13:** Let us learn, then, from Israel's errors in the wilderness so that we are not overtaken by the fate that overtook Israel. Israel's sin cost a whole generation the experience of life in the Promised Land. The eventual rest (in Canaan) into which Joshua led the people was not the final one, and many

lost even that temporary realm because of unbelief. A much greater Eternal Rest remains before us, and Jesus can lead us into it. We must take care that we do not lose it. Let us, therefore, watch, and encourage one another. We must never take our relationship with God lightly.

## THE SUPERIORITY OF JESUS' WORK
### Hebrews 4:14-10:18

Jesus is the High Priest of the new covenant. His work is superior to anything that preceded Him, and we must have an unwavering faith in Him. Jesus possesses the necessary qualifications for His office.

**1** **4:14–16:** Jesus is one with humanity and fully able to empathize with human frailties. We need have no overwhelming fears about our weaknesses, for we can appeal to a High Priest who understands us. Jesus knows our human condition perfectly, for He experienced suffering and temptation—although He did not yield to sin.

**2** **5:1–10:** The fact that Jesus was true man makes Him all the more effective as our High Priest. In the Old Testament experience, the High Priest was one with the people he served—he even shared their sin. Even so, he was appointed by God. Likewise, Jesus was appointed by God. Although He was God's Son, He learned obedience by walking the path of suffering. Jesus is a High Priest after the priestly order of Melchizedek and is able to save all humanity.

**3** **5:11–6:20:** The writer invites his readers to do more in-depth reflection on God's saving action in Jesus. Although he senses that they are not yet ready for it (5:11–14), he exhorts them to desire a more mature knowledge of Jesus, 6:1–8. He then balances his criticism by pointing to their past, and suggesting that there is good reason to believe that they will rise to the occasion and lay hold of their hope. That hope is based on God's promise and on Jesus' work as a High Priest. They should persist in hope—even as did Abraham of old, 6:9–20.

**4** **7:1–10:** Jesus belongs to a priestly order higher than that of Aaron. He belongs to the order of Melchizedek; see Genesis 14; Melchizedek, meaning *king of justice*; of Jerusalem, meaning king of *peace*, "*Salem*." When Abraham met Melchizedek, he gave him a tithe of all the booty he had recently captured. Melchizedek was a type of Christ, for his priesthood was unique and eternal; *Genesis makes no mention of his birth or death.*

The fact that Abraham (from whom came Aaron) gave tithes to Melchizedek points to the latter's superiority. Thus, the Levitical priesthood, through its ancestor Abraham, paid tithes to Melchizedck and, in doing so, acknowledged the superiority of his priesthood over theirs. Furthermore, the Levitical priesthood relied on succession to enable it to continue functioning over the centuries. However, no mention is made of Melchizedek's parents or his death.

**5** **7:11–14:** Perfection was not achieved under the Levitical priesthood. Had that been possible, there would be no need of a new priesthood. Not only that, but no new priesthood could come into existence without a change in the Mosaic Law the Levites served. However, Jesus did not come from *Levi*, but from *Judah*—a tribe never associated with the priesthood.

**6** **7:15–19:** Jesus carries out a priesthood that is based, not on family line, but on immortal existence and moral perfection. Therefore, Jesus abolishes the Levitical priesthood and the Law it served (neither of which was able to save!). Jesus now leads people into a direct relationship with God.

**7** **7:20–25:** Jesus' priesthood does not involve or require a succession; His High Priesthood is eternal and unchangeable. Jesus is able to save all who approach God through Him because He is an everlasting intercessor, and the guarantor of a permanent covenant relationship between God and humanity.

**8** **7:26–28:** Jesus is the High Priest people need. Jesus is holy and sinless, enthroned above all humanity, and does not need to perform repetitious sacrifices. Jesus achieved everything that was necessary when He sacrificed Himself once and for all. The Mosaic Law set up weak men as priests. God's promise and oath established His Son as the perfect High Priest.

**9** **8:1–7:** The Christian community has a High Priest who sits enthroned at God's right hand. Jesus presides over the heavenly sanctuary. He has something to offer (8:3; 9:12,14) that is different from the Levitical priesthood, which was a mere shadow of Jesus' mission and a mere shadow on earth of the perfect, heavenly offering.

**10** **8:8–13:** Jesus is the Mediator of a new and superior covenant that accomplishes what it signifies. Jeremiah already declared the old obsolete, Jeremiah 31:31–34.

The writer now compares Jesus' work with previous practices in the Old Testament Tabernacle. His descriptions are drawn largely from Exodus 25,26. All priests could enter the Holy Place, but only the High Priest could enter the Holy of Holies—which he did one day each year. The people were excluded from the Holy of Holies because their offerings could not obtain forgiveness but were merely symbols and tokens of their need of renewal.

**11** **9:1–14:** However, the true High Priest has entered the True Sanctuary—one not made by human hands. He is there permanently and has offered His own blood—blood that won eternal redemption for humanity. If the blood of animals could bestow ritual purification (through such fleshly things as food, drink, and ritual washings), how much more can Jesus' offering of His own blood accomplish? Jesus offered Himself to cleanse humanity *completely* and to equip it to render appropriate service to God.

**12** **9:15–28:** Jesus' role as the Mediator of the New Covenant resulted in His death. Even so, it freed people from sins committed under the old Mosaic covenant and made the people partakers of the New Covenant. As a will becomes effective only on the death of the one who made it, so Jesus' work in relation to the New Covenant became effective only by virtue of His death. Moses used blood to seal the Old Covenant (Exodus 24:1–8), for in the Old Testament guilt was removed through the shedding of blood. However, Jesus' death brought to finality Old Testament shadows. Jesus' death dealt with sin once and for all. It was the unrepeatable sacrifice.

**13** **10:1–18:** Old Testament sacrifices did not effect future spiritual benefits; they merely pointed forward to them. If they had brought about complete forgiveness, there would have been no need to repeat them. They were actually an ongoing reminder of the people's sin. Obviously, the blood of animals cannot remove sin. Jesus offered Himself for the very reason that He knew the inadequacy of the old sacrificial system. He offered one sacrifice, and this won Him a permanent place at the Father's right hand. He now awaits only the ultimate outcome of His work. He has brought about the New Covenant that makes all other sacrifices obsolete.

## EXHORTATIONS
### Hebrews 10:19–12:29

**1** **10:19–25:** We now have freedom of access into the presence of God through "the new and living way" Jesus has provided for us. Draw near to God in word and work.

**2** **10:26–31:** Beware of falling away or rejecting the redemption now offered. Those who abandon the true faith deliver themselves up to the judgment of God.

**3** **10:32–12:3:** Remember the steadfast faith that you demonstrated in former times. You stood firm despite hardships. Strive to do so again. Remember the examples of those who have gone before you. You stand in the succession of people of faith who accomplished great things. Look to Jesus, the pioneer and perfecter of your faith.

**4** **12:4–11:** Your present suffering is proof that God loves you. Remember that the Lord disciplines every child whom He receives.

**5** **12:12–29:** Repent while there is time—before it is too late. Seek to become strong in faith once again. God has spoken His word of grace to you. God's judgment is coming. Do not refuse what God offers. Do not refuse God's call. God is awesome!

**6** **13:7–19:** In the closing admonitions, the writer exhorts his readers to continue practicing brotherly love to strangers and prisoners, to refrain from immorality and greed for money, and to seek a contentment based on trust in God, 13:1–6. He urges them to keep in mind the example of their past teachers and to emulate their faith in Jesus, their opposition to false teaching, their firm break with Judaism, their sincere worship, and their earnest desire to do the will of God. They are to submit to their present leaders, obey them, and pray for them.

**7** **13:2–25:** The letter closes with a prayer, an appeal to heed the letter, news, a greeting, and a benediction.

**58A** Hebrews sets forth the superiority of Jesus' Person, and speaks of His work as the ultimate, once-and-for-all High Priest. The worship rituals practiced prior to Jesus' coming were but shadows of His final perfect work. Jesus does not minister in an earthly sanctuary, but in the perfect, eternal Heavenly Sanctuary. Because Jesus is also God's Son and King of the universe, God's people are to strive to live as members of His eternal people.

**58B** The contents of Hebrews reflect a personal relationship between the author and his readers. However, where they lived is uncertain.

With the exception of 1 John, Hebrews is the only New Testament letter to omit an opening greeting that mentions the writer's name. Down through the centuries, various suggestions concerning the author's identity have been made.

The letter to the Hebrews was most likely written to Jewish Christians who were growing lax in their faith and being tempted to revert to Judaism. It is possible that they were being ridiculed by fellow Jews who pointed to the weakness of Jesus in that He finished up on a cross. Although they had previously shown courage in crisis, they were growing faint in their struggle with sin. The writer exhorts them to remain firm in their faith. Jesus will empower them to overcome their spiritual weariness and faintheartedness.

Some date Hebrews prior to A.D. 64—just before Nero's persecution. Others suggest a date shortly before 70 A.D. when Jerusalem and its Temple were destroyed. Others again suggest a date from A.D. 80–90.

The central theme of Hebrews is that the Jewish sacrificial system is obsolete and has been superseded. The true worship of God is now linked to the saving work of the one-and-only authentic High Priest, Jesus the Messiah.

**58C** The writer sets out to demonstrate the superiority of Jesus' Person and work. As a *Person*, Jesus is superior to the angels and Moses.

Jesus' *work* also is superior. As the divine/human New Covenant High Priest, Jesus offered up Himself as the once-and-for-all atoning sacrifice for the sins of the world. His priesthood is the perfect fulfillment of the order of Melchizedek. It was established by an oath from God, is unaffected by death, and is unmarred by sin. Jesus understands His people perfectly, for He shares their human nature. By virtue of what He has done, His people have access to the very presence of God.

Those who belong to Jesus are to seek earnestly to do God's will while they wait for their High Priest to reappear from the Heavenly Sanctuary to receive them to Himself. They are to repent daily.

Numerous exhortations are contained in chapters 10 through 12. In the final chapter of the letter, the writer exhorts his readers to:

- continue practicing brotherly love to strangers and prisoners;
- refrain from immorality and greed for money;
- seek contentment based on trust in God;
- follow the example of their past teachers;
- resist false teachers and the temptation to revert to Judaism;
- seek at all times to know and do the will of God;
- submit to their present leaders, obey them, and pray for them.

# CROSS WAYS

**6 SECTION**

**UNITS 51–60**

## The Letters and Revelation

## UNIT 59

### 1 and 2 Peter; James; Jude

*Examining the Nature of True Discipleship*

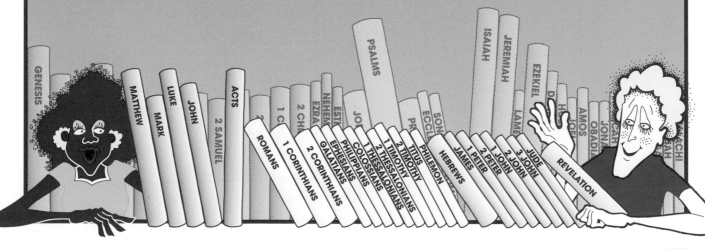

# First Peter: a Central Theme

**ILLUSTRATION 59A** depicts the situation to which Peter was speaking, and what Jesus' role as "example" implied for the people of Peter's day (and what it continues to imply for Christians today).

**1** Peter wrote his First Letter to Christians in Asia Minor. In **ILLUSTRATION 59A** (*lower center*), **one of these Christians is depicted with hands raised in praise**.

**2** These Christians were enduring difficulties. People within the community were ridiculing them because of their faith (**hostile face**, *lower left circle*). The threat of a Roman persecution hovered on the horizon (**Roman helmet and sword**, *lower right circle*).

**3** When advising the Christians of his day concerning how to deal with their challenging situation, Peter pointed them to the example of Jesus' suffering. He writes:

> *For to this you have been called, because Christ also suffered for you, leaving you an <u>example</u>, so that you should follow in His steps.* (1 Peter 2:21)

**4** Still today, some school rooms for children at grade school level are equipped with a white-board or a chalkboard—sometimes with the alphabet written in perfect script across the top. Students are encouraged to study this model alphabet, copy it, compare their efforts with it, and try to do better next time. In Greek, the word for this model alphabet is *hupogrammos*—the same word Peter uses, which we commonly translate simply as <u>example</u>. When we understand the word to mean more than merely an example—but rather, a perfect model to be studied and emulated—we perhaps get closer to the essence of Peter's intended meaning.

**5** Peter stresses that the model for the Christian's life is ***Jesus' servant life***—not the commandments given in Exodus 20 or Deuteronomy 5. Any Old Testament commandment repeated in the New Testament serves as a guideline for reflecting the servant life of Jesus. Christians are to make visible the servant life of the invisible but ever-present Jesus in all they think, say, and do.

**6** Peter's appeal is therefore: "Study Jesus' life constantly. Remember that Jesus always did His Father's will and served others as His Father wanted them served. Keep comparing your life with His, and keep striving to make your life more like His."

1.  In the opening address and greeting of his first Letter, Peter reminds his readers of the exalted origins of their faith and what it implies for their walk through life, 1:1,2. They are "chosen and destined" by the *Father* and "sanctified" by the *Spirit* "to be obedient to *Jesus Christ*." A number of times in what follows, whenever the letter mentions what God has done for humanity in Christ, it continues with a statement about the obligation God's action places on humanity.

    a.  We have been ransomed, not with silver and gold, but with the precious blood of Christ, the Lamb without blemish or spot. Therefore, we must be obedient children, 1:13–21.

    b.  We have tasted the kindness of the Lord. Therefore, we must put away all evil things, 2:1–3.

    c.  We have received the mercy of the Lord. Therefore, we must live like a holy people, 2:9,10.

    d.  Jesus has suffered for us. Therefore, we must leave the sins of the past behind, 4:1–6.

    e.  The end is near. Therefore, we must demonstrate a love that befits those who are stewards of God's grace, 4:7–11.

2.  First Peter is often called the letter of hope. It calls people to firm and serene dependence on God based on the certainty of the future resurrection that began, and is guaranteed, in the resurrection of Jesus the Messiah, 1:3–5.

3.  Our salvation is all God's doing. God alone is to receive the praise for what has come to pass, 1:3,5. God saved us through Jesus—the perfect Passover Lamb, 1:19. Jesus rescued us from our sin and the death it deserves through the shedding of His blood. Jesus is the Suffering Servant who brought healing and forgiveness to the world through His suffering on the tree of the cross, 2:21–24.

4.  God makes us members of His family through the regenerating waters of baptism. Baptism is more than a rite of initiation. It is a divine act in which the life-giving power of the glorified Jesus is communicated to the believer. It has a corporate dimension to it, for by it one becomes a member of God's *people*, a chosen *race*, a royal *priesthood*, and a holy *nation*, 2:9,10. Baptism places a person into a *saving* relationship with God and into a *serving* relationship with others. This serving relationship demonstrates itself in the following ways:

    a.  Where one partner in marriage is not a believer, the life of the Christian partner must be a silent, powerful, and irresistible sermon. Those who will not listen to the *spoken* word are to be won by the *lived* word, 3:1–6.

    b.  In daily work, a Christian is to reflect the spirit of Jesus, even when being subjected to cruel and unjust treatment, 2:18–25.

    c.  Within the community, the Christian's life is to make liars out of those who level condemning accusations, 2:11–17.

5.  To those being ridiculed because of their faith and facing severe persecution, the letter says:

    a.  Persecution is to strengthen, not destroy, those in Christ. God's people are to emerge from the experience like gold tried in the fire—with a faith so purified and strengthened that nothing can break it, 1:6,7.

    b.  The best answer to give lying accusers is not one of words, but that of a Christ-like servant life, 2:12.

    c.  Suffering is inevitable for the people of God. However, suffering must result only from *allegiance to Jesus*, not from *evil actions*, 3:13–17. After the cross comes the crown; after the suffering comes the reward of grace, 4:12–19.

All passages listed in this section are from First Peter, unless otherwise indicated. After an opening greeting (1:1,2), Peter reminds his readers of the significance of their baptism.

## AN EXHORTATION BASED ON BAPTISM
### 1 Peter 1:3–4:11

**1** God has given you salvation and new life; rejoice in it! (1:3–12)

Praise God that in mercy He has given new life and hope. God's gift is based on the resurrection of Jesus. Jesus' saving mission promises not merely an *earthly land*, but an *eternal inheritance in heaven*. God guards those who—through faith—are to receive it, and will reveal it to them on the Last Day, 1:3–5. Suffering and death preceded Jesus' resurrection. Similarly, trials go hand in hand with the walk to which the new life of faith calls us. We who are to receive the fullness of salvation in the *life to come* must expect to experience suffering in *this life*, 1:6–9. The Spirit of Jesus was active in the prophets to *predict* the salvation to come, and in the apostles to *proclaim* it, 1:10–12.

**2** Demonstrate your membership in the Chosen Race and Royal Priesthood! (1:13–2:10)

a. Be as ready ("prepare your minds") to meet Jesus as the fathers were to flee Egypt, 1:13. You once walked in ignorance of God, and this produced godless behavior. Your new relationship with God through Jesus is to produce holiness, 1:14–17. A high price was paid for your salvation—the blood of Jesus, 1:18–21. Now that you know the truth in Him, love one another with a fervent love, 1:22. Your rebirth into the new life is not the result of natural human processes, nor the product of human seed. The seed that produced it is the Word of God, 1:23–25.

b. Live up to your high calling! Strip off anything contrary to Jesus, and long for the Spirit's food that will empower you to grow in Christ, 2:1–3. Jesus is the Cornerstone of God's new Temple. As the Spirit joins new believers to Jesus, the Spirit incorporates them into this new, divine edifice as "living stones" who are to reflect the servant life of the Servant Cornerstone, 2:4–8.

c. Old Israel was once considered the chosen and elect race. You who form the new Israel can now lay claim to those titles. You are a "royal priesthood," formed to worship God and serve God's people. You are a "holy nation" set apart for God. In the new order of things, all genetic and national boundary lines are gone. God has now formed one community in and around Jesus. Now that you belong to this new community, you are to praise the God who delivered you from the darkness of paganism and made you sharers in the eternal light of God's salvation. You who were once "*not* a people" now *are* a people. You who were once without mercy now know God's mercy, 2:9,10; see Hosea 1:6–9; 2:23.

**3** Demonstrate your faith in practical ways (2:11–3:12).

a. Behave in a godly manner among those who do not know Jesus. Remember that you are strangers and exiles on earth—on your way home to the eternal Promised Land. Behave in a way that will move others to join you in your faith journey, 2:11,12. Obey those in positions of authority. In obeying them, you obey and serve God, 2:13–17.

- *Slaves*, imitate Jesus in the service of your masters. Jesus endured and suffered as He did to free us from our own sinful whims that we may serve the will of the living God, 2:18–25.

- *Wives*, remember your duties to your husbands, 3:1–6.

- *Husbands*, show love and consideration to your wives, 3:7.

b. The best way to ensure answers to your prayers is to take these admonitions seriously. Christian wives are to try to win an unbelieving husband to faith in Jesus by dressing themselves in the qualities of Jesus' life, and by copying the example of pious saints of old, 3:1–7. All must live together in a manner that contributes toward harmony, 3:8–12.

**4** Meet harassment and persecution God's way (3:13–4:11).

a. Conduct yourselves in a manner that will shame those who persecute you. By His suffering and death, Jesus, the righteous One, saved the unrighteous. Through His resurrection, He obtained life in the Spirit. We share this new life with Him through our baptism. Baptism is not designed to wash away *dirt* from the outer body, but *sin* from the inner person. An ark once saved Noah's family. Similarly, the waters of baptism now save those who would otherwise perish. Hence, we who have been joined to Jesus in baptism need have no fears about what others might do to us. We can live with a hope that transcends such fears. We can even rejoice in suffering and so cause our accusers dismay. Our posture in suffering might well encourage those who persecute us to inquire about the hope we hold precious, 3:13–22.

b. As Jesus suffered in the flesh, we Christians are to expect suffering as well. Have nothing to do with the pagan way of life under any circumstances. Those who yield to pagan vices must one day give account of their actions to the Lord, 4:1–6.

c. Jesus will return soon enough. While you wait for Him to come, demonstrate a calm demeanor; it will greatly enhance your prayer life. Practice love toward one another. Demonstrate sincere hospitality. Use whatever gifts God gives you to glorify God and to serve one another, 4:7–11.

## ADDITIONAL ADVICE TO THOSE BEING PERSECUTED
### 1 Peter 4:12–5:11

**1** If you have to suffer because of Jesus, rejoice! You share Jesus' lot, and His Spirit will rest on you. As you now share Jesus' suffering, you will ultimately share His glory. However, if you suffer because of your sins, that suffering will only be a foretaste of a punishment to come—and a deserved punishment at that, 4:12–19.

**2** Those who have been appointed elders to shepherd God's flock must fulfill their calling in a manner pleasing to God. Let your lives demonstrate what you proclaim. Do not be motivated by unwilling compulsion or by the desire for money, or to flaunt your position. Rather, demonstrate kindness and generosity in all that you do, 5:1–5.

**3** Equip yourselves with humility, trust, a sober and alert attitude, and a strong faith to deal with Satan who seeks to destroy you. What you may have to suffer is the common lot of Christians everywhere. God will help you through whatever comes your way, 5:6–11.

## CONCLUSION

*Through Silvanus, whom I consider a faithful brother, I have written this short letter to encourage you and to testify that this is the true grace of God. Your sister church in Babylon (Rome) chosen together with you, sends you greetings, and so does my son Mark. Greet one another with a kiss of love. Peace be to all of you who are in Christ.* (5:12–14)

# The Second Letter of Peter

## AUTHOR

Although the letter asserts (1:1) and suggests (1:16–18) that the apostle wrote it, that claim has long been disputed. Origen (A.D. 185–225) and Jerome (A.D. 342–420) questioned it. The work was accepted into the New Testament canon in the fourth century. All passages in this section are from Second Peter, unless otherwise indicated.

**1** The main reason for questioning the claim to authorship by Peter is what the letter has to say about the return of Jesus. In 3:1–13, it deals with the problems many Christians were having about the delay of the *parousia* (Jesus' final *appearing*). Most likely it was only around and after A.D. 70 (when the Romans destroyed Jerusalem and the Temple) that Christians began to adjust their thinking to the realization that the *parousia* was probably a long way off, and felt the need to explain the situation.

**2** The references in 3:2,4 suggest a post-apostolic dating.

**3** There is a close connection between 2 Peter and Jude. Jude is known to be a late writing. The literary relationship between the two suggests that 2 Peter was written after Jude.

**4** 2 Peter 3:15,16 refers to Paul's writings as though they had already been collected as Scripture.

**5** There is a marked difference in style and vocabulary between 1 and 2 Peter.

**6** A date in the post-apostolic period need not detract from the letter's inspired quality. Its message deserves careful attention.

## PURPOSE

The letter gives no hint as to where, or to whom, it was written. The suggestion that it was written to Gentile Christians in Asia Minor is as good as any. The writer's concern is that his readers should not forfeit their promised entry into the eternal kingdom of Jesus the Messiah in the coming Day of the Lord, 1:11. He stresses that he is not telling them anything new, but is merely reminding them of what they have already been taught, 1:12; 3:1,2. His message is not a subtle exposition of theology, but a trumpet blast. He wants to make his readers aware of the dangers they face from those who live Godless lives (ch. 2) and ridicule the idea of Jesus' reappearing, chs. 1 and 3.

## CONTENTS

The letter's opening address and greeting give no indication as to *where*, or to *whom*, it was written, 1:1,2.

**1** **An Exhortation to Christian Virtue** (ch. 1)
   a. The Christian life is a gift of power that God gives in grace to those whom He calls. This divinely given power brings us to *faith* in Jesus which, in turn, makes us sharers in the divine nature and equips us to resist the evils abounding in the world, 3,4. To your faith in Jesus, add the *virtue* of a distinctively Christian life, and to that the *knowledge* of how and why you should act, and to that the *self-control* that makes you a better servant of others, and to that the *steadfastness* that turns tragedy into triumph, and to that the *godliness* that makes all life an act of worship, and to that the *brotherly affection* that seeks harmony with all, and to that the *love* that seeks the well-being of all, 5–7. These are the fruits of knowing

Jesus. The person who lacks them walks in blindness, 8,9. We must take our calling and election seriously, for much is at stake—our entrance into God's everlasting Kingdom, 10,11.

b. It is important that I remind you of these things, for I have little time left in this world. I must soon die. I want to be sure you will remember these things after I am gone, 12–15. We share with you things we know to be true, things we saw with our own eyes—even on the Mount of Transfiguration. The truth we proclaim serves as a light to a world steeped in darkness. Keep your eyes fixed on that light until the eternal day dawns, 16–18. The prophets of old pointed to its coming. But beware! Private, flippant interpretation of the Scriptures is not permissible. The sacred writings are not a human product; they are the result of the Spirit's inspiration, 19–21.

**2**    **The Condemnation of False Teachers** (ch. 2)

There were false prophets in former times, and there will be again. In fact, they are already at work. They will deny the faith, give rise to immorality and scandal, and heap contempt on the way of salvation, 1–3. Be warned! God's ways of dealing with the evil and the righteous remain constant. Bear in mind how God dealt with the rebellious angels, people prior to the flood, and those who lived in Sodom and Gomorrah, 4–8. The false teachers presently at work are slaves to the flesh. They deny all outside authority—even that of the heavenly beings, 9–11. They act like brutish animals, 12. They are completely decadent and self-indulgent in behavior, 13. They conduct a never-ending search for more sin to commit, 14. Their eyes are constantly on the lookout for weak-willed women to seduce, 14. Like Balaam of old, they walk only in the paths that lead to financial gain, 15,16 (see Numbers 22–24). They drag down people who have just overcome some sin, and so make their latter condition worse than the first, 17–19. It would have been better for those people to have known nothing of Jesus than, once knowing the truth, to go back to their evil ways like a dog returning to its vomit, like a pig returning to its mire, 20–22.

**3**    **The Delay of the Lord's Return** (ch. 3)

Remember the truth you were once taught, 1,2. Bear in mind the approach that the false teachers adopt. They live immorally and deny both Jesus' return and the possibility of eternal retribution. They rationalize their behavior by claiming that Jesus has not returned, that many have died, and that the world is no better or worse, 3,4. Remember that God once destroyed the world with a flood. If God destroyed the world once, God can do it again—and will, 5–7. God does not perceive time as we do, 8. The reason for the delay in Jesus' return has to do with God's grace and patience. God's desire is to give more people time to repent, 9. But be assured that the Final Day will come with terrifying power and as unexpectedly as a thief in the night, 10. An awareness of these truths should make us conscious of our need to prepare, to watch, and to walk in the ways of God. So be ready at all times! Let there be no stain or defilement, and be at peace with one another, 11–14.

**4**    The letter closes with a reference to Paul's writings (15,16) and a closing exhortation, 17,18.

All passages listed in this section are from the Letter of James, unless otherwise indicated.

## AUTHOR

The author refers to himself as, "James, a servant of God and of the Lord Jesus Christ," 1:1. Several suggestions have been made about his identity.

**1** Some suggest that he was James, the son of Zebedee, the brother of John, Matthew 13:55. The fact that this James was martyred by Herod Agrippa I about A.D. 44 (Acts 12:2) makes this suggestion unlikely.

**2** In the early church, the opinion grew that the author was James, the brother of the Lord. This opinion contributed toward the work's reception into the New Testament canon. If the suggestion is correct, the letter came from an influential individual. He was an acknowledged leader in the church by A.D. 44, Acts 12:17. He played a prominent and authoritative role in the Apostolic Council, Acts 15:13–21. Paul reported to him at the conclusion of his third missionary journey and handed to him the contributions from the Gentile churches, Acts 21:18. Paul makes numerous references to him in his letters, 1 Corinthians 15:7; Galatians 2:9,12. His sphere of work seems to have been limited to the vicinity of Jerusalem. Tradition says he died a martyr's death in A.D. 62.

**3** Today, many have abandoned the suggestion made in point 2 above. They point out that the letter mentions Jesus only twice, 1:1, 2:1. It contains little reference to doctrines that are distinctively Christian. They suggest that the letter was originally a sermon used in a Jewish synagogue and was adapted for Christian use by the insertion of the name *Jesus* at 1:1 and 2:1. It was, therefore, written by an unknown James, or by someone hoping to gain acceptance for his work by referring to himself as he did.

**4** The position outlined in point 3 above might be rebutted as follows. The fact that the letter contains many Old Testament references proves little; the early church's Bible was the Old Testament. If the letter was not written by James of Jerusalem, how did it achieve such recognition? If an unknown writer was seeking recognition for himself, why did he not refer to himself as "James, the apostle," or "James, the brother of the Lord"? The writer's presumption in addressing "the twelve tribes of the Dispersion" (1:1), and his authoritative tone, continue to persuade many that he was indeed James of Jerusalem, a brother of Jesus.

## DESTINATION AND DATE

**1** The letter's address (1:1), and strongly Judaistic tone suggest that it was written to Jewish churches—possibly in Judea, Samaria, Galilee, Syria, and Cilicia. The letter contains no attack on sexual license, which was usually a problem in *Gentile* churches.

**2** Some date the letter as early as A.D. 45. They believe that it was written while the church was still predominantly Jewish—before Paul's work began. If they are correct, James is the earliest New Testament writing. Others believe that it attacks those who were distorting Paul's teachings about the relationship between grace and works, and was therefore written just prior to James' death in A.D. 62.

## OCCASION

**1** It is difficult to pinpoint the immediate reason for writing. The letter's illustrations are general. It makes no reference to Jewish/Gentile tensions. However, 1:2 refers to "trials of any kind," and 5:19,20 addresses a closing admonition about those "who wander from the truth." Apparently the recipients were suffering under the twin pressures of poverty and persecution. The temptation to become depressed and impatient was strong, and the prospect of many succumbing to the ways of the world was real, 5:19,20.

**2** Those who believe that the letter was written at an early date suggest that it was written to the church whose history is outlined in Acts 1–12, a church still enmeshed in Judaism and still a part of historic Israel. The term translated "assembly" (2:2, RSV and NRSV) means "synagogue"; early Christians continued to worship in synagogues.

## TONE

**1** The letter contains 108 verses, of which 54 contain imperatives or commands. The writer reminds his readers that faith must not be abstract, but must express itself in every aspect of life. The letter makes no reference to heresy. The only danger facing the readers is that caused by the imperfect and perverse behavior of those who claim allegiance to God.

**2** James has an obvious Old Testament tone. Some of it reads like wisdom literature. Jesus' words have left their mark on the author's mind, even though he never quotes them directly. There are obvious similarities between James and Matthew; compare James 2:13 with Matthew 5:7; James 3:12 with Matthew 7:16; James 3:18 with Matthew 5:9; James 5:2,3 with Matthew 6:19–21.

**3** The letter's lively and vivid style captures the attention and imagination. The language is concrete and clear, and contains a number of little narratives (5:7, a farmer waiting for his harvest), and vivid, verbal sketches (2:2,3, the reaction when a rich man enters an assembly). James confronts his readers with searching questions, commands, and direct address. Even so, his concern is not to demonstrate his facility with words, but to impress upon his readers the need to exhibit sincerity of faith through a life of obedience.

**4** James makes use of colorful imagery. As he develops his message, he refers to the stars of heaven, the sea and the wind, the fields and the sun, the fig tree and vine, the early and latter rain, the process of harvest, fountains, the morning mist, the birds, beasts, fish and creeping things, the forest and forest fire. It would seem that James had an eye for the world of nature. Perhaps his style was influenced by the sayings of Jesus.

## CONTENTS

**1** **Meet Trials God's Way** (1:2–18)

Greet them with joy. Remember that testing gives opportunity for endurance, and endurance gives opportunity to achieve greater perfection, 2–4. The person who prays for wisdom to achieve endurance and perfection receives it; he who doubts does not, 5–8. Human opinions about the value of being rich or poor do not count before God; God's way of evaluating things is the reverse of human opinion. Riches have the lasting capacity of a meadow flower subjected to the sun's fierce heat, 9–11. He who persists faithfully in the way of Jesus, no matter what the cost, receives the crown of life, 12. God tempts no one to do wrong; people's passions entice them. When they yield to these passions, the result is sin. The result of the passion-enticement-sin cycle is death, 13–15. What we become in relation to God is the end result of God's work in us. God is beyond all change. Through His Word, God desires to bring about a new birth in our lives and to make us the first-fruits of a new creation, 16–18.

**2** **Make Sure That Your Worship Is Sincere** (1:19–27)

God desires us to respond to His Gospel readily, to accept it promptly, and to fashion our lives to conform to it. God wants us to remove from our lives anything that might hinder our spiritual growth, lest His Word encounter some obstacle in us, 19–21. The person who hears God's Word but does nothing about it misunderstands completely God's intentions about how life is to be used. True happiness is the by-product of conforming to God's law of true freedom, 22–25. Sincere faith must demonstrate itself in control of the tongue; in concern for the needy, the defenseless, and the oppressed; and in avoiding the world's polluting influence, 26,27.

### 3 Give Due Respect to the Poor (2:1–13)

A Christian must not discriminate against the poor or show favoritism to the rich. Those who fail in this respect operate with a value system that is the reverse of God's value system. Those who abuse the poor dishonor Christ. The person who fails to love and serve the neighbor breaks the whole of God's Law. God's people are to bear in mind that there is a final judgment; that thought should move them to take His will seriously.

### 4 Faith without Works Is Dead (2:14–26)

Although people are never saved *by* works, they are saved *for* works. There is little value in merely professing that God exists. The demons believe that—and tremble at the thought, 14–19. Remember Abraham's example. He certainly believed that God existed. However, he demonstrated his faith by being prepared to offer his own son as a sacrifice. *A living faith demonstrates itself in loving actions, in deeds of service, and in compassion for others. A dead faith lacks all these signs of life*, 20–26.

### 5 Teachers Must Learn to Control Their Tongues (3:1–12)

Although the tongue is small, it is the instrument that conveys teaching. The bit placed into a horse's mouth is small, as is also the rudder on a ship, but both achieve great things. Similarly, the tongue: It has a great potential for harm—like that of a tiny spark to start a forest fire.

It is possible to tame many things on this earth, but virtually impossible to control the tongue. It is the cause of so much harm. All too often blessing and curse come out of the same mouth. The words that flow across a tongue indicate the moral health of the body they leave.

### 6 Teachers Must Not Give Way to Arrogance (3:13–18)

Those who are wise do not fall victim to selfish arrogance. The person who is endowed with gifts from on high demonstrates this through purity, love of peace, consideration for others, sweet reasonableness, sincerity, mercy, and kindness. By way of contrast, earthly wisdom demonstrates itself in sensual cunning, demonic jealousy, strife, and worldly greed and ambition.

### 7 Friendship with the World Means Enmity with God (4:1–12)

Some ask, "Why do conflicts raise their ugly head in the Christian community?" The answer is that they result from the misuse of the tongue and from the false wisdom that is a by-product of love of the world. Remember that the world is always at war with God. Conflicts can also result from the misuse of prayer—which often means the total neglect of prayer, or using it to satisfy one's own whims. God wants praying people to focus on submission to God and His will, repentance, humility, and the fight against evil.

### 8 Submit to God's Will in Every Situation (4:13–17)

Life is at the best of times a very uncertain affair. Who can be sure what *tomorrow* might bring, let alone *next year*? Our life-span is short. If we wish to live triumphantly, we must commit our lives to God. If we do not, we are guilty of arrogance and presumption.

### 9 Strive after True Riches! (5:1–20)

What value, what permanence, is there in those things that you have spent life accumulating? Your victims' cries are heard in heaven itself! You will be destroyed together with your trinkets.

Those who have been exploited by the rich are to bear their lot patiently and to fix their eyes on the salvation that they will eventually receive. As they endure their difficult lot in life, they are to bear in mind the example of the prophets and saints of old, 5:7–11. Do not resort to the use of glib oaths, 12. Always pray fervently for yourselves and for others, and confess your sins to one another. Remember that fervent prayer is indeed effective, 13–18. Be alert to those who stray, and bring them back to the proper path in life. A saved soul is a precious thing indeed, 19,20.

1

2

**1** The Letter of James did not receive general recognition in the church until the fourth century because the church was not sure who wrote it. The question about James' right to a place in the New Testament canon was raised again at the time of the Reformation—not only by Luther, but also by Roman Catholic scholars. Luther based his objection to James chiefly on 2:14–26. He felt that it was virtually impossible to reconcile this passage with Paul's insistence that salvation is by grace, through faith, without the works of the Law.

**2** However, there is little reason to believe that James contradicts Paul's teaching. Most likely, James is attacking what Jesus attacked when He said that the teachers of Judaism *professed* but did not *practice*, Matthew 23:3. It is reasonable to suggest that the misconceptions that plagued Judaism plagued early Christianity as well.

**3** The suggestion that James is attacking Paul is disproved by the fact that James' bold but simple presentation would have been a very weak refutation of Paul's teaching. Both simply emphasize different aspects of the one salvation.

    a. Paul stresses that salvation is wholly a gift of God's grace and entirely God's doing; faith receives what God gives.

    b. James stresses that faith unites us with God and commits us to seek to know and do His will. It rejects the notion that faith is merely the intellectual acceptance of doctrinal statements.

**4** Paul spoke to the sinner's *plight*. James spoke to Christian *complacency*. To understand what is involved, it is important to be familiar with biblical thinking patterns as they apply to the relationship between God's grace and human response. **ILLUSTRATION 59F** helps clarify the issue. Its lower center section depicts the six parts of the covenant formulations described in **ILLUSTRATION 8C** and **ILLUSTRATION 56B**.

- Preamble
- Historical Prologue
- Commandments (or stipulations)
- Preservation and re-reading
- Witnesses
- Blessings and curses

    a. In this covenant pattern, God *first* declares who He is, and *second* spells out what He has done for His people. Only then does God define the manner in which His people are to respond to His gracious acts on their behalf.

    b. **ILLUSTRATION 56B** serves as a reminder that Paul uses this thought pattern in his letters. For example, in Ephesians 1–3 Paul states who God is and what God has done for His new people. In Ephesians 4–6 Paul spells out how God's people are to respond to the divine grace that has been lavished on them. The sequence is invariably: *Indicative—Imperative.*

The segments at the *top left* and *top right* of **ILLUSTRATION 59F** depict how people can abuse, or be confused about, God's relationship with them.

**1** *Top left:* There are people who profess faith in God (**_first dot in circle_**) and make reference to God's saving acts (**_second dot_**). However, because they then do what they please, rather than what pleases God, their attitude is *all grace, no response*—an attitude that leads to *presumptuousness.* James deals with this matter in 2:14–26; Paul deals with it repeatedly, e.g., Romans 6:1–4.

**2** *Top right:* Some people see salvation as a matter of *all works—no grace* (**symbol for commandments in circle**). This can produce either pride or despair—*pride*, because they want God and others to notice how much good they do (see Paul's answer to this in Romans 2:17–3:20); *despair*, because they know they are lost and condemned sinners and don't know what to do about it (see Romans 7:21–26; 8:31–39).

In what follows, all quotes are from Jude, unless otherwise indicated.

## AUTHOR

**1** The author introduces himself as "Jude, a servant of Jesus Christ and brother of James," v. 1. This statement identifies him as the brother of James, the brother of Jesus, James 1:1. Jude, like James, had not believed in Jesus during His earthly ministry, John 7:5. His name is listed in Mark 6:3 and Matthew 13:55. Luke refers to these brothers as a group, and associates them with the Twelve during the period of the early church in Jerusalem, Acts 1:13. Nothing is known about Jude's history.

**2** It is not known to whom the letter was addressed, nor from where it was written. In view of the fact that Jude refers to the apostles as having belonged to a time now past, it is suggested that the work was written about A.D. 70.

## CONTENTS

**1** The church was being troubled by a form of Gnosticism similar to that referred to in 1 and 2 John. Its emphasis was not on *asceticism* (*living an austere life*), but on *antinomianism* (*belief that there are no moral absolutes*). James felt compelled to write to deal with the problem, vv. 3,4.

**2** Jude exhorts his readers to remember at all times how God deals with those who rebel against Him. He refers to the fate that overtook those Israelites who rebelled in the wilderness after the exodus event, the angels who wanted to go their own way, and Sodom and Gomorrah, vv. 5–7.

**3** The false teachers refuse to submit to authority of any kind. They walk in the ways of Cain, Balaam, and Korah. They defile the flesh, slander the angels, ridicule whatever they do not understand, and exercise a corrupting influence at love-feasts. They are like clouds that promise refreshing rain, but produce none. They are like trees that give a show of leaves, but bear no fruit. They are as effective as roaring waves that expend themselves only to produce froth and foam. They are like stars to which sailors look for guidance, only to receive none, vv. 8–13.

**4** These grumbling, discontented, bombastic, flattering deceivers need to bear in mind the judgment that Enoch of old predicted would overtake them. God will come with an angelic host to judge and convict them, vv. 14–16.

**5** God's people are to heed the predictions and warnings of the apostles. They are to protect themselves from the threat the false teachers pose by building themselves up in the faith, praying in the power of the Holy Spirit, keeping themselves in the love of God, and waiting for the Final Day of history. They must abhor all false teachers and strive to rescue those ensnared by them, vv. 17–23.

**6** There is One who stands ready at all times to preserve God's people in the true faith—God Himself, vv. 24,25.

**59A** If the Old Testament law-codes no longer serve as guidelines for Christian living, who or what does? In his first letter, Peter speaks of Jesus as the *example*, the model for the godly life. The word he uses for "example" refers to the perfect line of writing across the top of a chalkboard that students are to continue to study and copy as they learn to write and to improve their writing skills. The heart and core of Peter's appeal is, "Study Jesus' life constantly. Keep comparing your life with His, and keep striving to make your life more like His life."

**59B & 59C** The *First Letter of Peter* was addressed to Gentile Christians in Asia Minor. It was written in Rome about A.D. 63–64, just prior to the outbreak of Nero's persecution. Pagans were making life difficult for God's people, and the prospect of persecution lay ahead. In urging God's people to rejoice in their sufferings, Peter reminds them that, as they share Jesus' sufferings on earth, they will also share His glory in heaven. In suffering as they do, they are experiencing the common lot of Christians throughout the world. They are to live Christ-like lives at all times and in every circumstance. By doing this, they bear witness to their Lord and shame those who are making life difficult for them.

The letter can be understood as an exhortation based on Baptism. It contains some of the clearest statements about Baptism in the New Testament. It assures God's people that their hope in relation to participation in the life to come is sure. Those who have come to faith in Jesus are to reflect Him in all that they do. The best way to deal with lying tormenters and accusers is not to attack them with words, but to show them the Jesus that God wants them to believe in. Although God's people will endure difficulties in life, suffering must result only from allegiance to Jesus, not from evil actions. After the cross comes the crown!

**59D** Many question the Petrine authorship of the *Second Letter of Peter* and suggest that it was written in the late first or early second century. The book deals with a situation in which some within the outward Church are denying Jesus' Second Coming (Final Reappearing), and are claiming that the possession of God's forgiving grace gives them the right to do as they please. The writer wants to make his readers aware of the dangers they face from those who live godless lives and ridicule the idea of Jesus reappearing. The letter exposes the motives of the false teachers, affirms the prospect of Jesus' final reappearing, and exhorts its readers to sincere faith and earnest discipleship.

**59E** The *Letter of James* was most likely written by a brother of Jesus who played a prominent role in the life of the early church, particularly in Jerusalem. It is possible that his letter was the first New Testament writing. Its tone suggests that it was written to Jewish churches whose members were suffering poverty and persecution. James urges his readers to meet trials God's way, to engage in sincere worship, to show compassion to the poor, to control their tongues, to reflect a humble demeanor, to submit to God's will at all times, and to be aware of the dangers involved in seeking to become rich.

**59F** Some see Paul and James making contradictory statements in their writings. Not so!

- Paul devotes considerable energy to defining faith in Jesus as Messiah and Savior, and the implications of following Jesus as Servant Lord.
- James attacks those who profess the Christian faith but do not practice discipleship. His basic theme is, "Faith without works is dead."
- Paul speaks to the sinner's *plight*; James speaks to the sinner's *complacency*.

**59G** The *Letter of Jude* was written to counteract a certain antinomian heresy ("use life as you please") that had wormed its way into the Church and was twisting the concept of Christian freedom. Jude warned his readers that the ways of God do not change; divine judgment overtakes all who flagrantly flout God's truth and will.

# CROSS WAYS

## 6 SECTION

### UNITS 51-60
## The Letters and Revelation

## UNIT 60
### The Revelation to John

*Words of Hope to God's Threatened People*

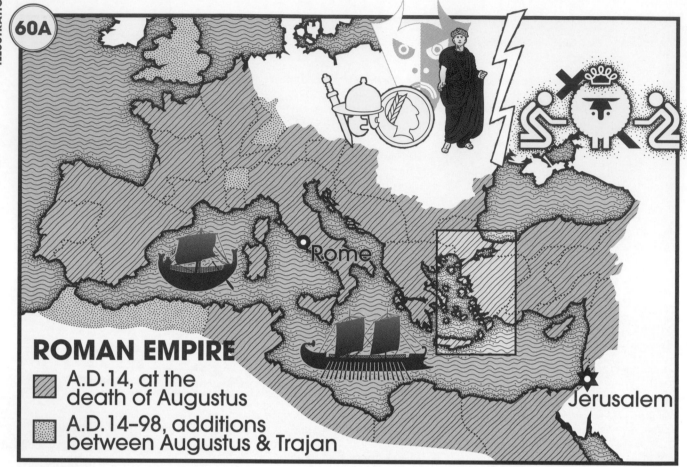

## ROMAN EMPIRE

A.D. 14, at the death of Augustus

A.D. 14–98, additions between Augustus & Trajan

© H. N. Wendt 2007

## Revelation And Rome

The author of Revelation states that his name is John (1:1,4), that he is a servant of God (1:1), one of the prophets (22:19), and a brother who shares in the tribulation of his readers, 1:9. He says that he wrote while on the island of Patmos to which he has been exiled because of his faith, 1:9. He is familiar with the cities of western Asia; they are not far from the island to which he has been banished.

Tradition has it that the writer was one of the Twelve disciples and that, in addition to Revelation, he wrote the fourth Gospel and the three Johannine letters. However, many scholars dispute the Johannine authorship of Revelation. They suggest that Revelation contains so many Hebraic and Aramaic expressions and so much bad grammar that it could not have come from the pen of the writer of the fourth Gospel and the Johannine letters.

Revelation, like the book of Daniel, speaks to an historical situation. God's people, whose focus is on events that culminated in Jesus' crucifixion and resurrection in *Jerusalem*, are facing the threat of persecution by *Rome*. The author sees Rome as the embodiment of emperor worship, which to accept is to deny the sovereignty of God. The "beast" that symbolizes the empire is the agent of Satan.

Revelation exhorts its readers not to fight against Rome; God will soon bring about its fall. God's people are to see their situation as a prelude to the Final Appearing of Jesus when they will be vindicated and all earthly authority will be destroyed.

**ILLUSTRATION 60A** provides information about the Roman imperial system that the writer of Revelation sees as posing a serious threat to the people of God.

1. The borders that were in place when Caesar **Augustus** died in **A.D. 14** were extensive.

2. Although the empire continued to expand beyond A.D. 14, only a limited amount of territory had been added by the time that **Trajan** became emperor in **A.D. 98**.

3. Roman **trading ships** (*vessel at left*) transported supplies from around the Mediterranean Sea to Rome and other major centers.

4. Roman **naval vessels** (*vessel at right*) sought to ensure the empire's security, and to deal with piracy at sea.

5. In the *top right section* of the illustration are symbols of the opposing powers with a **fragmentation symbol** between them.

   ● Rome (*at left*): **Roman helmet and sword, coin; emperor clad in purple robes**.
     Behind these symbols is a **demonic face**. (The writer linked the imperial system to Satan.)

   ● God's people (*at right*): **crowned Lamb of God** (Jesus) **with cross; servant figures**.

6. The **rectangle** over the west of Asia Minor (present-day Turkey) and the east of Greece depicts the region in which the seven churches addressed in Revelation 2,3 were located. (See 60F.)

## Emperor Worship

1. In form, Revelation is a letter—complete with an opening salutation and a closing benediction, 1:4; 22:21. Although it is addressed to *seven churches* in the Roman province of Asia (1:4), it speaks to the *whole first-century church*. The work describes the situation that called it forth: God's people are being threatened by a persecution (1:9) that has already cost some their lives (2:13, 6:9,10), and are being troubled by false teachers, 2:6,14,15.

2. Why were the early Christians being persecuted? They were refusing to take part in emperor worship.

3. What did emperor worship entail? In the early days of the empire, many worshiped the spirit of Rome. They did this to acknowledge that Rome had brought peace and justice to the world. The spirit of Rome was said to be incarnate in the person of the emperor. The empire was extensive: from Britain to the Euphrates, from the Danube to North Africa. What principle was used to tie this vast domain together? The answer was: *Caesar worship.* This did not mean that attempts were made to destroy every other faith and to make emperor worship the exclusive faith. However, all people in the empire were expected to burn a pinch of incense to the emperor once a year and to declare, "Caesar is Lord!" After doing this, they could worship as they pleased.

4. When the emperor cult was propagated in the province of Asia, a collision was bound to take place between the cult and God's people. For Christians, Jesus alone was Lord. Nothing and no one on earth could make them say, "Caesar is Lord!" Their refusal to participate in the requirements of emperor worship made them appear to be disloyal citizens. Revelation speaks to this situation. Two themes run through it:

   a. Those suffering are to persevere in the faith, and are assured that they will be vindicated and rewarded.

   b. God will intervene to judge and punish those who are afflicting God's people.

# Persecution: When, and How Much? 60C

To what degree did God's people suffer Roman persecution during the first century A.D.?

**1** Some believe that Revelation was written during the reign of Nero (A.D. 54–68). However, Nero's persecution was carried out in the immediate vicinity of Rome. There is evidence that, beyond the time of Nero, local and sporadic harassment *sometimes* led to persecution or even martyrdom. However, there is little reason to believe that an *empire-wide* persecution took place during the decades that immediately followed.

**2** The early Church father, Irenaeus, wrote that Revelation was written toward the close of the reign of the emperor Domitian, A.D. 81–96. Domitian was the first emperor to make an issue out of emperor worship. It was during his reign that Christians *throughout the empire* found themselves living under threat—albeit not full-scale persecution at this point.

**3** Most modern scholars agree that Revelation was written during the last days of Domitian—about A.D. 95. Revelation sees whatever persecution was taking place as an indicator that a world-wide persecution of God's people would soon break out, and that the persecution would precede the coming end of history.

**4** An *empire-wide, empire-sponsored* persecution of Christianity began only about the middle of the third century A.D. during the reign of the emperor Decius, A.D. 249–51.

**5** Although some see Rome as the sole or major enemy in Revelation, it is important to note that Acts points to the comparatively friendly attitude of Romans toward Christians experiencing Jewish hostility. Furthermore, some of the attacks on believers mentioned in the Letters to the Seven Churches are attributed, not to the Romans, but to Jewish hostility, Revelation 2:9.

# Decoding Revelation

**1** Today, many readers are puzzled by Revelation's symbolism—and even disturbed by its bloodthirsty images and expressions of hatred. Some read it with the desire to determine the precise date of Jesus' reappearing and the end of the world. Some have identified the evil beings it depicts with historical figures such as Napoleon and Hitler.

**2** The majority of present-day biblical scholars interpret Revelation in light of the historical situation prevailing when it was written—during the last years of the first century A.D. They believe that is a letter intended to be read in the churches to which it is addressed (see 60E). It is an *apocalyptic* writing—a style of writing that was popular between the Testaments and common in Jesus' day. (The Book of Daniel is such a writing; see Unit 38.) Although several New Testament writings *contain* apocalyptic images, Revelation is the only example of an *entire* apocalypse in the New Testament.

**3** There are, nevertheless, certain differences between Revelation and typical apocalyptic. Apocalyptic works were pseudonymous (written under a pen-name); John wrote in his own name. Apocalyptic had speculative interests and sought to calculate the times and seasons of the world's last days and its end. John does not attempt to satisfy curiosity about such matters. His goal is to give hope and courage to those facing the prospect of persecution. Concerning the end time, he simply reports Jesus' words, "Surely I am coming soon," 22:20.

**4** The details of the visions in Revelation are not to be taken literally. How can a person visualize a lamb with seven horns and seven eyes? Yet such terms are used to describe Jesus, 5:6. The point is that the seven horns and seven eyes *represent* something—Jesus' universal power (*seven horns*) and universal knowledge (*seven eyes*). Similarly, in Revelation colors and numbers have symbolic meanings (144,000 = immensity; 1,000 = a large number; 12 = Israel's 12 tribes or the 12 apostles; 7 = perfection; 6 = imperfection; 4 = the world).

**5** Since about the middle of the 19th century, some within Christendom have linked Revelation's references to "Gog and Magog" (20:8) and "Harmagedon" (16:16), sometimes spelled "Armageddon," to supposed end-time events. These interpretations are invalid; each term is used only once in the New Testament—in the passages listed. Gog and Magog are referred to in Ezekiel 38,39 (addressed to the exiles in Babylon) where the message is that God will lead the exiles back to Judah and finally destroy all Gentile rulers and powers that seek to harm them. "Harmagedon" (which means "the hill of Megiddo") has links to present-day Megiddo on the edge of the plain of Jezreel. After the Israelites entered the land under Joshua, many battles were fought there. Revelation uses the name *symbolically* when referring to the final destruction of those who were harassing God's people—with "those" referring to those who, in John's day, embraced the beliefs and practices of the Roman imperial system. To read into these passages (and 1 Thessalonians 4:13–17 and Revelation 20:2–7) an end-time theology of "rapture, Armageddon, and millennium" is to be misled.

# Revelation in Outline

It is difficult to construct a satisfactory outline of Revelation, for the work contains doublets, artificial constructions, and repetitious elements. The writer did not set out to systematize doctrine, but to stun his readers with images and visions. Revelation is a carefully structured work in which the number seven plays a central role. The book's contents may be summarized as follows:

| | | |
|---|---|---|
| **Introduction** (1:1–20) | | |
| 1 | 1:1–3 | Source and purpose |
| 2 | 1:4,5a | Greetings |
| 3 | 1:5b–8 | Jesus the Messiah's past, present, and future work |
| 4 | 1:9–20 | John's inaugural vision on the island of Patmos |
| **The Seven Letters** (2:1–3:22) | | |
| 1 | 2:1–7 | Ephesus |
| 2 | 2:8–11 | Smyrna |
| 3 | 2:12–17 | Pergamum |
| 4 | 2:18–29 | Thyatira |
| 5 | 3:1–16 | Sardis |
| 6 | 3:7–13 | Philadelphia |
| 7 | 3:14–22 | Laodicea |
| **The Seven Seals** (4:1–8:1) | | |
| | 4:1–11 | The setting in heaven: |
| | | ● God enthroned in glory |
| | 5:1–14 | ● The scroll and the Lamb |
| 1 | 6:1,2 | First seal: white horse |
| 2 | 6:3,4 | Second seal: red horse |
| 3 | 6:5,6 | Third seal: black horse |
| 4 | 6:7,8 | Fourth seal: green horse |
| 5 | 6:9–11 | Fifth seal: martyrs beneath an altar |
| 6 | 6:12–17 | Sixth seal: cosmic signs; many seek to escape from God |
| | | *Two supplementary visions:* |
| | 7:1–8 | ● Marking of 144,000 on earth |
| | 7:9–17 | ● The elect before God's throne |
| 7 | 8:1 | Seventh seal: silence in heaven |
| **The Seven Trumpets** (8:2–11:18) | | |
| | 8:2–6 | The setting in heaven: seven angels with trumpets; signs in nature |
| 1 | 8:7 | First trumpet blast: a third of the earth is burned |
| 2 | 8:8,9 | Second trumpet blast: a burning mountain thrown into the sea |
| 3 | 8:10,11 | Third trumpet blast: a burning star falls into the sea |
| 4 | 8:12,13 | Fourth trumpet blast: a third of the sun, moon, and stars darkened |
| 5 | 9:1–12 | Fifth trumpet blast (first woe): deadly locusts, bottomless pit |
| 6 | 9:13–21; 11:14 | Sixth trumpet blast (second woe): angels, army, destruction |
| | | *Two supplementary visions:* |
| | 10:1–11 | ● The angel with the little scroll |
| | 11:1–13 | ● Measuring the Temple; the two witnesses |

| | | |
|---|---|---|
| 7 | 11:14–18 | Seventh trumpet blast (third woe): God's Kingdom breaks in |

**The Seven Signs** (11:19–15:4)

| | | |
|---|---|---|
| | 11:19 | The setting in heaven |
| 1 | | First sign: |
| | 12:1–6 | ● The woman and the child |
| | 12:7–12 | ● Michael and the dragon |
| | 12:13–17 | ● The dragon pursues the woman |
| 2 | 13:1–10 | Second sign: the beast from the sea |
| 3 | 13:11–18 | Third sign: the beast from the land |
| 4 | 14:1–5 | Fourth sign: the 144,000 and the Lamb |
| 5 | 14:6–13 | Fifth sign: three proclamations |
| 6 | 14:14–20 | Sixth sign: three voices proclaim messages |
| | 15:1 | *A supplementary vision:* Seven angels with seven plagues |
| 7 | 15:2–4 | Seventh sign: sea of glass |

**The Seven Bowls** (15:5–16:21)

| | | |
|---|---|---|
| | 15:5–16:1 | The setting in heaven |
| 1 | 16:2 | The first bowl: sores afflict those who worship the beast |
| 2 | 16:3 | Second bowl: sea turns into blood; all life within it dies |
| 3 | 16:4–7 | Third bowl: rivers and springs turn into blood |
| 4 | 16:8,9 | Fourth bowl: sun's heat scorches the godless |
| 5 | 16:10,11 | Fifth bowl: beast's throne and kingdom enshrouded in darkness |
| 6 | 16:12 | Sixth bowl: Euphrates river dries up |
| | 16:13–16 | *A supplementary vision:* demons set stage for battle at Harmagedon |
| 7 | 16:17–21 | Seventh bowl: storms, hailstones; Rome splits, cities crumble |

**The Seven Sights** (17:1–20:15)

| | | |
|---|---|---|
| | 17:1–18 | Introductory: The harlot on the beast |
| 1 | 18:1–8 | First sight: two angels with messages |
| 2 | 18:9–20 | Second sight: kings, merchants, sailors, dirges |
| 3 | 18:21–24 | Third sight: Babylon (Rome!) is silenced |
| 4 | 19:1–10 | Fourth sight: God's people rejoice |
| 5 | 19:11–21 | Fifth sight: victory over the beast and false prophet |
| 6 | 20:1–3 | Sixth sight: the dragon is chained |
| | 20:4–10 | *A supplementary vision:* God's elect reign for 1,000 years during the period of Satan's release |
| 7 | 20:11–15 | Seventh sight: final judgment |

**The New Creation and New Jerusalem** (21:1–22:5)

| | | |
|---|---|---|
| 1 | 21:1–8 | The voice from the throne |
| 2 | 21:9–22:5 | A vision of the Heavenly Jerusalem |

**Epilogue** (22:6–21)

| | | |
|---|---|---|
| | 22:6–20 | Final attestations |
| | 22:21 | Final blessing |

The above outline reveals that Revelation contains six major segments that are "book-ended" by opening and closing sections, 1:1–20, 22:1–21. Some suggest that the fact that there are six major sections (one short of the perfect "seven") declares that perfection will surface only in the coming Eternal Age. It is also significant that in the six major sections (each with seven parts) there are seven supplementary visions.

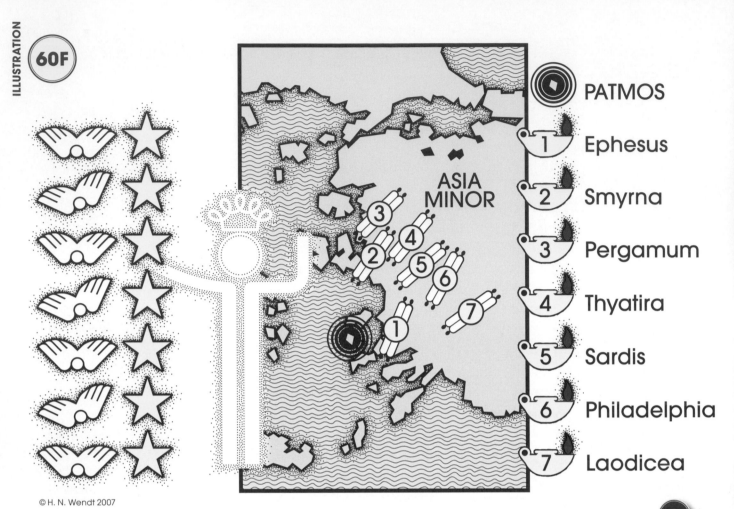

© H. N. Wendt 2007

PATMOS

1 Ephesus

2 Smyrna

3 Pergamum

4 Thyatira

5 Sardis

6 Philadelphia

7 Laodicea

## Introduction; The Seven Letters

**60F**

### Revelation 1:1–3:22

**ILLUSTRATION 60F** depicts the locations of **PATMOS** and the **seven churches** to which the seven letters (**seven scrolls**) are addressed. It also contains **seven stars**, and symbols of **seven angels** and **seven lamps**—all referred to in the book's first chapter.

## INTRODUCTION

### Revelation 1:1–20

 The opening chapter provides information about the character, destination, and purpose of Revelation. The book is a "revealing" of the work already accomplished, and being accomplished, by Jesus the Messiah to the glory of the Father and to the benefit of humanity. The sequence of persons involved in revealing these truths is: God the Father to Jesus, to an angel, to John, to the reader, to the hearer. The writer says that he received his revelation on the island of Patmos where he was imprisoned "on account of the word of God and the testimony of Jesus." (Patmos was used by the Romans as a penal colony.) The chapter contains:

    a.   A prologue that defines the **source and purpose** of Revelation, 1:1–3. John assures his readers that the time of Jesus' reappearing is near—a comforting thought for Christians who are suffering.

    b    **Greetings**, 1:4,5a.

    c.    Information about **Jesus the Messiah's past, present, and future work**, 1:5b–8.

    d.    **John's inaugural vision on the island of Patmos**, 1:9–20.

**2** In 1:4a, John begins by giving his name. (Nowhere in Revelation is John called an apostle, nor is he identified with the Twelve.) He states that he received a divine vision on the Lord's Day while on the island of **PATMOS**, 1:9. He then makes reference to the seven churches in Asia that he addresses in chs. 2,3; see 1:10,11. These churches were located in seven major cities in western Anatolia (present-day Turkey) in the Roman province of Asia. They are listed in a circle—from south to north and back again. All were within 100 miles (160 kilometers) of **Ephesus**.

**3** John prays that "grace" and "peace" be bestowed on his readers by God the Father ("who is and who was and who is to come") and Jesus the Messiah. Some find a reference to the Holy Spirit and the various energies of the Spirit in the words "the seven spirits who are before the throne"; see Isaiah 11:2ff. Others believe these words refer to the seven archangels who stand before God, 3:1; 4:5; 5:6; 8:2. (When John wrote, the Jewish belief was that communities on earth have their counterparts in heaven among the angels.)

**4** Three titles are ascribed to Jesus: "the faithful witness" (or martyr), "the firstborn of the dead," and "the ruler of the kings of the earth," 1:5. In 1:5b–8, Jesus' past, present, and future work is summarized.

**5** In 1:9–20, John's preparatory vision on Patmos is outlined; 1:20 interprets 1:12,16 in which **lampstand** is a symbol for "church" and **star** is a symbol for "**angel**." John sees the exalted and eternal **Jesus the Messiah** standing in the midst of the seven churches. Awesome, majestic roles and qualities are ascribed to Him by means of symbols: priesthood, royalty, eternity, strength, and omniscience, 1:12–16.

**6** Terms that express victory over death are ascribed to the "one like the Son of Man" whom John saw, 1:13. He is "the first and the last, the living One," the One who was dead but now lives forever, the One who holds "the keys of Death and Hades," 1:17,18.

**7** The fact that it was Jesus who spoke through John would have brought joy to John's readers, for they were living under the shadow of the threat of death. Jesus spoke through John to inform them about those things that would take place before and after His reappearing.

## THE SEVEN LETTERS

### Revelation 2:1–3:22

The seven letters are not letters in the usual sense of the word, and lack opening greetings and closing salutations. They resemble the edicts and decrees issued by Persian kings and Roman emperors. Their purpose is to encourage their readers to remain loyal to Jesus the Messiah in the face of persecution from without and temptation from within. They are addressed to the churches at Ephesus, Smyrna, Pergamum, Thyatira, Sardis, Philadelphia, and Laodicea. Apart from the church at Ephesus, established by Paul, this passage is the only place in the New Testament where we are given information about Christian life in the other six centers. However, the number "seven" is a symbol of perfection and completeness that is meant to represent the entire Church. Although each congregation has its own letter, each letter is intended for all "the churches."

The author has a good knowledge of the setting and tradition of each city, and a specific message for the church in each of them. Three of the churches are warned against false teachers, referred to as Nicolaitans. Although little is said about their vices, they are linked with Balaam (Numbers 22–25) and Jezebel (1 Kings 21 and 2 Kings 9:30–37) and accused of advocating sexual licence and eating food sacrificed to idols. Even so, the general picture is of peaceful and well-established groups that are in danger of complacency and succumbing to the temptations of their religious and social environment.

 **Ephesus** (2:1–7): In the letter to the Christians at Ephesus, Jesus

   a.   *praises* them for their endurance, for bearing up under persecution, and for testing the orthodoxy of their teachers;

   b.   *reproaches* them for losing their first love; and

   c.   *promises* them that they will eat of the tree of life in the heavenly paradise.

Ephesus, with a population of about 250,000, was the most important city in Asia. It was the hub for a series of roads to significant areas of Asia Minor. The imperial cult was established there about 29 B.C. when a temple was built for the worship of the goddess Roma and the deified Julius Caesar. Within the city was an amphitheater that seated 50,000 people. Ephesus was the capital for the imperial cult at the time of Domitian.

 **Smyrna** (2:8–11): In the letter to the Christians at Smyrna, Jesus

   a.   *praises* them for standing firm despite tribulation, poverty, and slander;

   b.   *offers* no reproaches; and

   c.   *promises* them the crown of life and preservation from the second death.

Smyrna, the "flower of Asia" and a magnificent trade city (with a harbor to the west), was rebuilt about 200 B.C. according to plans and designs attributed to Alexander the Great. In 195 B.C., its citizens built a temple to the goddess Roma. In A.D. 26, they were granted the right to build a temple to the divine Tiberius and the Roman Senate—a privilege denied to all other Asian cities at that time.

 **Pergamum** (2:12–17): In the letter to the Christians at Pergamum, Jesus

   a.   *praises* them for remaining true to Him and standing firm in the faith;

   b.   *reproaches* them for tolerating false teachers; and

   c.   *promises* them eternal life under the figures of hidden manna and a white stone with a new name on it.

Pergamum was not as famous in the business world as were Ephesus and Smyrna. However, Pliny praised it as the most famous city in Asia. Its library housed about 200,000 scrolls and was second in size only to that in Alexandria. (The writers and librarians in Pergamum invented parchment.) It was the principal locality for Caesar worship in the province of Asia. On the slopes of a hill overlooking Pergamum were temples to Zeus, Athena, and Asklepios. Asklepios, the god of healing, brought thousands to the city each year; he was referred to as "the savior," and his emblem was a serpent. An immense white marble altar (now in the Pergamum museum in Berlin), dedicated to Zeus, was part of the temple complex. The Roman governor stationed there was permitted to use the sword to inflict capital punishment to enforce the "Caesar is lord" law.

 **Thyatira** (2:18–29): In the letter to the Christians at Thyatira, Jesus

   a.   *praises* them for their faith and love, and their growth in service;

   b.   *reproaches* them for heeding false teachers, practicing immorality, and eating food offered to idols; and

   c.   *promises* them that they will share His Messianic rule.

Thyatira served as a military outpost for Pergamum. It had no proper acropolis, no famous cult, no gods of note, and was not an official center for Caesar worship. However, there were many workers' guilds within its walls: bakers, potters, brass-workers, tanners, leather-workers, wool and flax processors, clothiers, and dyers. When guild members met, they shared a banquet that often resulted in drunkenness and sexual immorality. Sometimes the meat served at a banquet had been sacrificed on pagan altars. Workers who refused to take part in these banquets faced social ostracism and financial peril.

**5** **Sardis** (3:1–6): In the letter to the Christians at Sardis, Jesus

    a.   offers *no praise*;

    b.   *reproaches* them for their spiritual deadness; and

    c.   *promises* the faithful among them that they will be clothed in white, that their names will stand in the Book of Life, and that He will confess their names before the Father and His angels.

Sardis had once been a symbol of great wealth, splendor, and power. At the time when Revelation was written, it was no longer that. It was not a government center, nor the base for any special industry. No special gods were worshiped within its walls. However, it remained a large and prosperous city.

**6** **Philadelphia** (3:7–13): In the letter to the Christians at Philadelphia, Jesus

    a.   *praises* them for having remained loyal to Him and for keeping His Word;

    b.   offers *no reproaches*; and

    c.   *promises* them that they will be pillars in the Temple of God and that He will write new names on them.

Philadelphia was founded with the express purpose of being an open door for Greek culture to the regions of Lydia and Phrygia. It was located in a region that was subject to severe earthquakes. Because of the dangers posed by collapsing buildings and falling objects, the city's residents lived in constant fear and were always ready to flee to safety outside the city's walls.

**7** **Laodicea** (3:14–22): In the letter to the Christians at Laodicea, Jesus

    a.   offers *no praise*;

    b.   *reproaches* them for being lukewarm, complacent, and self-satisfied; and

    c.   *promises* them that He will share table with them and they will sit on His throne.

Laodicea, founded in the middle of the third century B.C., was located at the crossroads of commerce and trading ventures from east to west and north to south. It was named after its founder, Laodice, the wife of the Seleucid king, Antiochus II. It served as a banking center, as a manufacturing center for woolen outer garments, and as a center for the manufacture and export of eye and ear ointments. It was situated on the Lycus River. Across the river and to the north were mineral springs whose waters flowed over white lime-encrusted cliffs.

To comfort and encourage Christians facing or suffering persecution, John held before them a vision of the glory that would finally be theirs. He also assured them that their persecutors would eventually reap their just reward. It would have been easy for John's readers to conclude that a day of reckoning awaited the evildoers, and that only a glorious future awaited them. The Seven Letters reminded John's readers that they, too, must constantly examine themselves lest they become blind to their own sins and weaknesses. The abuses referred to applied to all seven churches, even as they apply to the church in every generation. Similarly, the rewards promised to one church were available to all, even as they are available to all Christians to the end of time.

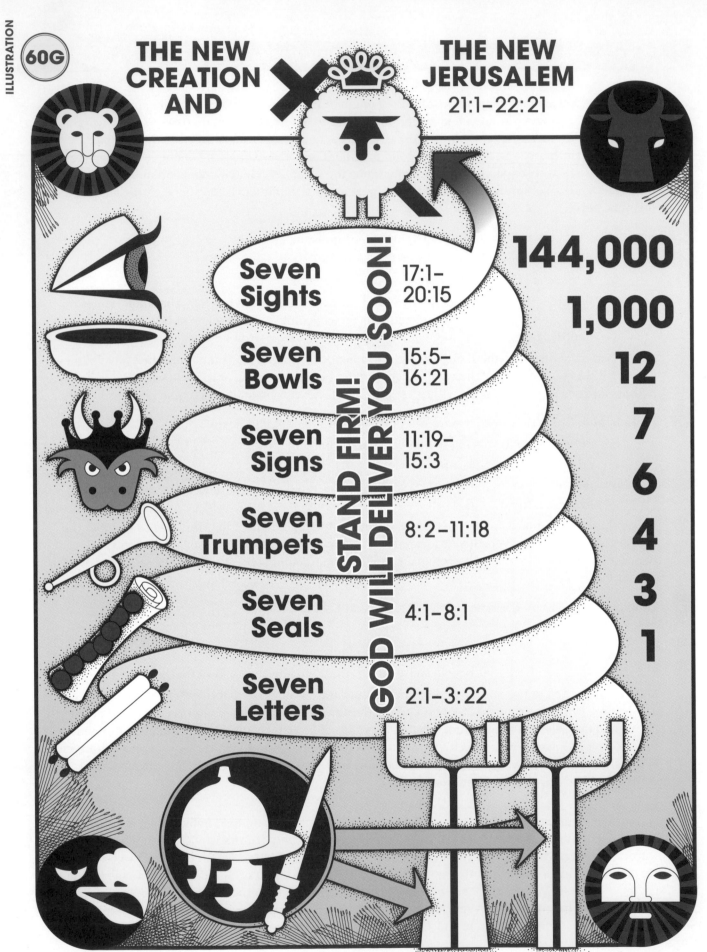

Revelation is a Semitic writing. Its message moves in circles rather than in a straight line. With the exception of the first major section (The Seven Letters), each unit spans the whole period between the present and the reappearing of the Lord, and each unit sets forth the same truth. However, each unit introduces a new aspect of the basic theme. Progression does occur as the vision of the end is portrayed with increasing fullness. The writer loves his central theme and never tires of repeating it. He tells of the petitions of the Christians being persecuted, the divine response, the plagues of punishment as God intervenes, and the heavenly bliss of the redeemed. And then he starts the cycle all over again! He bids his readers to be ready to hear the same message numerous times.

**ILLUSTRATION 60G** depicts the "big picture" in the Revelation to John.

**1** *Roman helmet and sword; arrows pointing to the right; crowned Lamb of God, cross, two servant figures:* John wrote to Christians facing the threat of persecution and martyrdom at the hands of Roman authorities.

**2** *STAND FIRM! GOD WILL DELIVER YOU SOON!* These words constitute the central message of hope that runs through Revelation. Despite outward circumstances, Christians can feel secure because Jesus the Messiah, once slain, is now the victorious Lamb of God, the King of the universe, and the Lord of history.

After the introductory chapter and the letters to the seven churches in chapters two and three, Revelation assures the persecuted Christians that God is enthroned in the heavens and is in control of His universe. In His permissive will, God allows certain difficulties to overtake His people during their walk through this life. However, God will soon deliver and vindicate them, and destroy their foes.

**3** *Rising spirals:* John emphasizes his message of comfort and assurance not just once, but numerous times. He does this by means of a spiraling series of visions, each built around the number *seven* and each incorporating one or two supplementary visions. The final vision is that of the New Creation and the New Jerusalem.

**4** The illustration summarizes the visions and their location in Revelation, and depicts some of the symbols John employs to present his message in the successive sections:

- four beasts (represented by the heads of a *lion*, an *ox*, a *man*, and an *eagle*);
- *scroll* (denoting the seven letters to the churches in Asia);
- *scroll with seven seals*;
- *trumpet*;
- *beast* (similar to those referred to in Daniel and Ezekiel 1);
- *bowl*;
- *eye* (signifying "sights");
- numbers (*1, 3, 4, 6, 7, 12, 1,000, 144,000*)

**5** The use of numbers in Revelation reflects the numerology that was common in Jewish writings and in the Greco-Roman world. The basic numbers are three, four, and seven which signify completeness and perfection, as 12 (three times four) represents the 12 tribes of Israel and the 12 apostles of Jesus. When reading through Revelation we note the following use of numbers:

- seven letters, chs. 1–3;
- seven seals, 5:1;

- seven visions, seven bowls of wrath, 16:1;
- seven angels and seven trumpets, 8:2;
- three disasters ("woes", chs. 9–16) are followed by the final deliverance that increases three to four;
- four living creatures around God's throne, 4:6;
- four destructive horsemen, 6:2–8 (four is derived from the "four winds").

The "New Jerusalem," the perfect Messianic city, has 12 gates for the 12 tribes (21:12) and 12 foundations for the 12 apostles (12:14). The number 12 is also the basis for the dimensions of the New Jerusalem: a 12,000 stadia long cube (1,500 miles by 1,500 miles by 1,500 miles—or 2,400 kilometers cubed) surrounded by walls 144 cubits high (12 times 12 cubits—about 215 feet, or 65 meters), 21:16,17. There are 24 elders (chs. 1–3) and 144,000 elect (12 times 12 times 1,000)—12,000 from each of the 12 tribes of Israel, chs. 4–8.

The famous "number of the beast" (666, Revelation 13:18) is an example of the writer's use of numbers as "code" to communicate his message. The number 666 is obtained by adding up the mathematical value of the *Hebrew* letters that translate *Kaisar Neron*—the *Greek* for "Emperor Nero" (Qsr Nrwn: Q = 100; S = 60; R = 200; N = 50; R = 200; W = 6; N = 50; total = 666). According to a widespread legend, Nero had not really died (in A.D. 68) but would soon return with a great army from the East, 13:3. The list of seven kings, of whom five have fallen (17:9,10), may refer to the chaotic conditions in the Roman empire after Nero's death; there were five emperors in the space of a year. The larger message is: Although the Roman emperor might claim divine status (as Nero did), he is merely an imperfect human being.

## THE SETTING IN HEAVEN

### Revelation 4,5

The section relating to the seven seals is introduced by an inaugural vision in heaven, 4:1–5:14. (Events in heaven determine what is to take place on earth; see also 7:9–17; 8:1–5; 11:15–19; 14:2,3; 15:2–8; 19:1–10; 21:3–8; note also 1 Kings 22:19–23 and Job 1:6–12.) The purpose of the vision is to create an impression of the overwhelming glory of God, and the majesty and authority of Jesus the Messiah in relation to the unfolding of history. **ILLUSTRATION 60H** depicts some of its details.

**1** *Symbol for God, throne:* John is taken up into heaven where he finds himself in sublime company; he sees God on a heavenly throne. Although God's Person is not described, the splendor of God's presence is depicted in terms of dazzling stones and a brilliant halo. God's throne is placed on, and surrounded by, spectacular phenomena, 4:5,6a. Thunder and lightning issue forth from the throne, and seven torches burn in front of it. A sea of glass resembling crystal spreads out before it. In describing God's throne, John's purpose is to paint a picture of God's divine glory and transcendence. God's presence is of such shimmering magnificence that it is beyond comparison with anything on earth.

The One on the throne holds in His hand a ***scroll with seven seals***, 5:1. Standing beside the throne is a ***Lamb*** with seven horns and seven eyes (5:6) who takes the scroll, removes each of its seven seals, and foretells what is to take place as history unfolds, 5:6 (see *THE SEVEN SEALS* below for more detail).

**2** *Twenty-four crowns:* Around the central throne is a circle of 24 thrones, on each of which is an elder clad in white and wearing a golden crown.

Various suggestions are made concerning the significance of the twenty four elders, e.g., the twelve tribes of Israel and the twelve apostles. Perhaps John is suggesting that if the central throne is surrounded by such splendor and by so many dazzling attendants, how immeasurably great is the One seated on it!

**3** *Four faces, eyes:* Around the throne are four living creatures, 4:6b; see also Ezekiel 1:4–14.

Each has six wings. Each is covered with eyes—to signify God's constant awareness and watchfulness. Each appears as a different creature to signify God's…

- awesomeness (*lion*),
- strength (*ox*),
- wisdom (*man*), and
- mobility (*eagle*).

Each of the 24 elders and four beasts holds a harp and a bowl of incense which they use to praise God and the Lamb ("Holy, holy, holy") and bow before them as they do so, 5:8–10.

**4** *Angelic beings (wings):* The assembly continues to grow, 5:11. Beyond the circle of the 24 elders and their thrones is a second circle of myriads and myriads and thousands of thousands (many millions) of angels. They join the 24 elders and four beasts in praising the Lamb, 5:12.

**5** *Outer circle of people in community:* Beyond the second circle is a third, consisting of every creature in heaven and on earth, and under the sea and in the sea. All join in praising the One on the throne and the Lamb, 5:13,14.

John's goal is to declare that God alone is the One from whom everything is derived and to whom all must be subject—and God has declared the Lamb to be the Lord of history.

**6** The ***bread and cup*** serve as reminders that, in the Eucharist, worshipers today continue to join with "angels and archangels, and with all the company of heaven," to offer praise to the Creator and Redeemer, and to celebrate that, by virtue of their faith in Jesus the Messiah's death and resurrection, they are already members of God's eternal family. The day will soon come when they will share in the marriage supper of the Lamb in the eternal, heavenly realm, 19:9.

## THE SEVEN SEALS

### Revelation 6:1–8:1

In 5:1ff., John introduces into his vision a ***scroll with seven seals*** and the Person of Jesus the Messiah (***Lamb, cross***). The scroll, which God holds in His right hand, contains the details of the future divine plan for humanity and the church. No one in the universe is thought to be worthy to remove the seals and to reveal the scroll's contents—until John's guide informs him that the Lion of the Tribe of Judah and the Root of David will do so. John then sees Jesus, as a ***Lamb*** that has been slain, with seven horns (symbols of strength) and seven eyes (symbols of watchful insight) standing in the immediate presence of His Father. Jesus takes the scroll from God's hand. At this point John sees the second and third circles of worshipers mentioned above. Their songs and praise are directed to both God and the Lamb.

The fact that it is Jesus who holds the scroll assures those being persecuted that their security and future are in good hands. The scene is now set for Jesus to remove the seals. The messages of the first six seals point to the divine judgments that will overtake the wicked.

**1** **First seal**, 6:1,2.
As Jesus opens each of the first four seals, one of the four living creatures shouts, "Come!" and a colored horse sets forth bearing a rider. The first horse is white. Its rider wears a crown, carries a bow, and goes forth to conquer. The vision represents warfare.

**2** **Second seal**, 6:3,4.
The second horse is red. Its rider carries a large sword symbolizing civil strife and death in battle.

**3** **Third seal**, 6:5,6.
The third horse is black. Its rider holds in his hand a pair of scales symbolizing famine.

**4** **Fourth seal**, 6:7,8.
The fourth horse is pale green, bears a rider named Death, and is followed by Hades. These figures symbolize famine, pestilence, and death. The destruction wrought by this horse and its rider is severe, but not total.

The four seals symbolize the course of history between the Ascension and the day of Jesus' reappearing. God permits the evils of war, death in battle, famine, pestilence, and disease to overtake humanity. However, these evils are under God's control; He sets limits to their effects. They serve as disciplinary punishments for those opposed to God, but create yearnings in the hearts of those who long for Jesus' reappearing.

**5** **Fifth seal**, 6:9–11.
John sees the slain martyrs praying for deliverance. They are given white robes and are exhorted to exercise patience until the number of those yet to be martyred and brought to the faith is complete.

 **Sixth seal**, 6:12–17.

John sees manifestations of seven apocalyptic phenomena that affect seven categories of men. The wicked seek relief from the misfortunes God inflicts on them through the forces of nature by attempting to flee and by seeking self-destruction.

John now includes *two supplementary visions*. In the *first supplementary vision* (7:1–8), John assures his readers that they will be spared these agonies. They need not fear the wrath of the Lamb, for He will be their Shepherd. John sees four angels holding back the destructive forces of nature to allow time for an angel to place a seal on those under divine protection; see Ezekiel 9:3–6 and note that, according to Jewish tradition, the control of nature was entrusted to angels. The number sealed is 144,000, or 12 x 12 x 1,000. The number is based on the traditional twelve tribes of Israel and is symbolic of the membership of the total church on earth; see also James 1:1 and Galatians 6:16. The term "sealed" occurs frequently in the New Testament, John 6:27; 2 Corinthians 1:22; Ephesians 1:13.

In the *second supplementary vision* (7:9–17), the scene changes from the church on earth to the church in heaven. John now sees a portrayal of the final outcome of the sealing action described in 7:1–8. A vast multitude, gathered from all parts of the earth, is assembled around the throne and the Lamb. Its members are clothed in heavenly garments and sing the praises of Him Who brought about their salvation. They have passed through the sufferings and tribulations of life on earth, and now wear robes washed white in Jesus' blood. God will dwell among them eternally. The blessings they enjoy in God's presence are described in meaningful earthly terms; see also Isaiah 25:8; 49:10. The "heavenly circles" described in 4:1–5:14 assent to the songs of praise the redeemed sing.

 **Seventh seal**, 8:1.

The meaning of 8:1 is uncertain. Perhaps it indicates that, because the scroll is now completely open, an awesome silence prevails in heaven as it waits for the destruction soon to be poured out on the enemies of the Lamb and His people.

**148**

**Revelation 8:2–11:18**

The setting is the Heavenly Court. John sees seven angels, each of whom is given a trumpet. Before the first angel blows his trumpet, John sees yet another angel rain fire from the heavenly altar on to the earth—heralding the devastation that will follow each trumpet blast, 8:2–6.

In the visions of this section, the Christian community appeals to God to vindicate His truth. God, in turn, reveals to them the desolations that will overtake the sinful world in which they bear witness. Trumpet blasts introduce visions of the coming calamities. (For references to the role of the trumpet, see Exodus 19:16,19; Isaiah 27:13; Joel 2:1; 1 Corinthians 15:52; 1 Thessalonians 4:16; Matthew 24:31.)

**1** **First trumpet blast**, 8:7,
followed by calamities affecting the vegetation.

**2** **Second trumpet blast**, 8:8,9,
followed by calamities affecting life in the sea.

**3** **Third trumpet blast**, 8:10,11,
followed by calamities affecting the waters of the earth.

**4** **Fourth trumpet blast**, 8:12,
followed by calamities affecting the atmospheric conditions.

An eagle then warns of the last three trumpet blasts, 8:13.

**5** **Fifth trumpet blast**—and the **first woe**, 9:1–12.
After the fifth trumpet blast, an invasion of evil spirits, under the image of a plague of locusts, results in the harassment of those without God's seal on their foreheads.

**6** **Sixth trumpet blast**—and the **second woe**, 9:13–21; 11:14.
After the sixth trumpet blast, a horde of demonic warriors destroys a third of humanity.

*Two supplementary visions* follow. These describe the preservation of God's people in the face of opposing forces:

- The angel with the little scroll, 10:1–11.
- The measuring of the Temple, and the two witnesses, 11:1–13.

**7** **Seventh trumpet blast**—and the **third woe**.
The seventh trumpet blast heralds the breaking in of God's kingdom, 11:14–19.

**Revelation 11:19–15:4**

Again, the setting is in heaven, 11:19.

**1** **First sign**, 12:1–17.
A dragon seeks to destroy a woman and her son, 12:1–6. The archangel Michael conquers the dragon, 12:7–12. The dragon vainly pursues the woman, 12:13–17.

**2** **Second sign**, 13:1–10.
The dragon bestows his power on the beast rising from the sea.

**3** **Third sign**, 13:11–18.
John sees a second beast, and the false prophet from the earth.

**4** **Fourth sign**, 14:1–5.
John sees a vision of the Lamb with His own—the 144,000.

**5** **Fifth sign**, 14:6–13.
John hears three angels proclaim imminent judgment.

**6** **Sixth sign**, 14:14–20.
John sees the nations being gathered for judgment.

Then follows a *supplementary vision* in which John sees seven angels holding the final seven plagues to be visited on humanity, 15:1.

**7** **Seventh sign**, 15:2–4.
John sees a heavenly throne room scene. Those who have overcome the beast and its image sing songs of praise to God.

The message is: The church, symbolized by a woman, brings forth Christ and is attacked by Satan—but in vain. Satan's forces then attack the heavenly angels, but are overcome and thrown down to earth where Satan gains partial control and attacks the church itself, ch. 12. Satan employs two beasts to act as his agents:

    a.    The *first*, a beast from the sea with ten horns, seven heads, ten diadems, and a blasphemous name symbolizes the political power of the Roman empire, 13:1–10.

    b.    The *second* is a beast from the earth who works together with the first beast to promote the worship of the Roman Emperor, 13:11–18. Most likely the reference is to the Roman priesthood that promoted and supported emperor worship.

The visions in Revelation 14:1–15:4 are designed to strengthen the suffering church and to assure it of the certainty of final victory.

# The Seven Bowls

## Revelation 15:5–16:21

The setting is in heaven, 15:5–16:1. The vision reflects that described in 4:1–11. Seven angels empty seven bowls, and bring on a succession of disasters—some of which resemble the plagues of Egypt.

**1** **First bowl**, 16:2.
Ugly sores break out on those who bear the mark of the beast, or worship its image. See Exodus 9:8–11.

**2** **Second bowl**, 16:3.
The sea turns to blood and every living creature within it dies. See Exodus 7:20,21.

**3** **Third bowl**, 16:4–7.
The rivers and springs turn to blood.

**4** **Fourth bowl**, 16:8,9.
The sun is given the power to burn people with its fierce heat. The victims blaspheme God.

**5** **Fifth bowl**, 16:10,11.
The fifth angel pours out his bowl on the throne of the beast. Its kingdom is plunged into darkness, and people bite their tongues in pain.

**6** **Sixth bowl**, 16:12.
The waters of the Euphrates dry up to prepare the way for the coming of the kings (Parthians) of the east (literally, "rising of the sun").

A *supplementary vision* follows, 16:13–16. Three foul spirits resembling frogs come from the mouth of the dragon, from the mouth of the beast, and from the mouth of the false prophet (identified with the two-horned beast, 13:11–18). The frogs (see Exodus 7:26–8:11) represent demonic spirits who gather together the kings of the world for battle on the great day of God the almighty.

**7** **Seventh bowl**, 16:17–21.
The seventh angel pours his bowl into the air. A loud voice from the Temple proclaims, "It is done!" Then come lightning flashes, rumblings, thunder, and a great earthquake. The great city splits into three parts, and the Gentile cities fall. God remembers the great Babylon (Rome), and gives it a cup filled with the wine of His fury and wrath. Islands flee and mountains disappear. Large hailstones fall on the people—who blaspheme God because the plague is so severe.

## Revelation 17:1-20:15

In this section, the judgment and fall of Babylon (Rome) are described. In an introductory vision, John sees a harlot seated on the beast, 17:1–18.

**1** **First sight**, 18:1–8.
John sees two angels who proclaim: Babylon (Rome) will fall! Leave the condemned city!

**2** **Second sight**, 18:9–20.
John witnesses lamentations over Babylon (Rome) by kings, merchants, and sailors.

**3** **Third sight**, 18:21–24.
A symbolic action depicting the destruction of Babylon (Rome).

**4** **Fourth sight**, 19:1–10.
John witnesses rejoicing in heaven over the fallen city.

**5** **Fifth sight**, 19:11–21.
Jesus is depicted as victorious over the beast and the false prophet.

**6** **Sixth sight,** 20:1–3.
Satan is bound.

A *supplementary vision* follows (20:4–10) in which John sees the redeemed reign for 1,000 years during Satan's time of release.

**7** **Seventh sight**, 20:11–15.
John witnesses the final, universal judgment. The section describes God's victory over His enemies, the destruction of Rome, the last judgment, etc. One must not read more into ch. 20 than it says. It does not speak about any millenial reign of Jesus on earth. The period of "a thousand years" (20:4,5) must be understood symbolically, as must other numerals in Revelation. The vision describes the preservation and security of Jesus' *martyred people*, from the day of His ascension to the day of His reappearing.

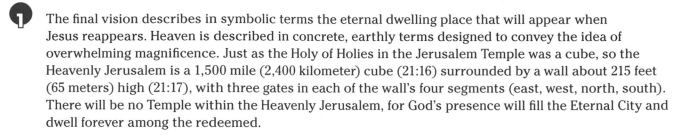

**Revelation 21:1–22:5**

**1** The final vision describes in symbolic terms the eternal dwelling place that will appear when Jesus reappears. Heaven is described in concrete, earthly terms designed to convey the idea of overwhelming magnificence. Just as the Holy of Holies in the Jerusalem Temple was a cube, so the Heavenly Jerusalem is a 1,500 mile (2,400 kilometer) cube (21:16) surrounded by a wall about 215 feet (65 meters) high (21:17), with three gates in each of the wall's four segments (east, west, north, south). There will be no Temple within the Heavenly Jerusalem, for God's presence will fill the Eternal City and dwell forever among the redeemed.

**2** A stream (referred to as "the river of life") flows from the throne of God and of the Lamb. On its banks are trees that produce fruit each month, and whose leaves serve as medicine for the nations; see Ezekiel 47:1–12. God's servants will worship Him and the Lamb. God's name will be on their foreheads, and they will look on God's face. Night will be a thing of the past. There will be no more need for lamp or sun, for God will provide His own with light and they will reign forever and forever.

## EPILOGUE

**Revelation 22:6–21**

In the closing epilogue, John refers to the witness of the angel (22:6–11), the witness of Jesus (22:12–20), and attaches a concluding blessing, 22:21.

Although Revelation states little that is new, it restates much that is old.

**1** God is keeping a watchful eye on the welfare of persecuted Christians. Although their life is being made difficult, those harassing them will have to suffer far more than they themselves ever have. At the same time, John reminds them that their own lives are under constant divine scrutiny, and there is much in the church that displeases the Risen Lord. He exhorts his readers to persevere in faith in God's grace and to practice a sincere love for one another.

**2** Revelation depicts the transcendence of God in vivid and concrete ways. God is enthroned above creatures that signify perfection. At the same time, God intervenes continually to bring about the salvation of humanity. Despite appearances to the contrary, God remains in control of all that happens. Secondary agents (war, famine, earthquake, disasters, etc.) play their roles according to God's good pleasure. Their purpose is to bring sinners to repentance.

**3** The Father gives to His Son authority to remove the seven seals so that history may run its course. Not Caesar, but Jesus, is Lord! Jesus abides among His own. Jesus walks in the midst of His church. The Father and Jesus are worthy of equal worship, 1:7,8,17; 5:13; 7:10; 19:16.

**4** Although Satan has been conquered and judgment has been pronounced on him, Satan will be confined to hell only when Jesus reappears on the Last Day of history. Until that time, Satan will continue to pursue the woman and her offspring. For reasons not stated, evil spirits are also permitted to trouble humanity in the intervening period.

**5** The work of redemption has been completed. However, God's people will receive their final inheritance only when Jesus reappears. Although God's people possess eternal life in *faith*, they enjoy it only in *hope*. While they wait to receive their promised salvation, they must be prepared to suffer the abuse of this world in patience. They find their strength and joy in the certainty that their Lord stands beside the throne of God and directs the course of history. Because Jesus has given them glimpses of the glory that awaits them, they pray with fervor: "Come, Lord Jesus!"

**6** Revelation contributes rich insights into the celebration of the Eucharist. In the Preface of the Eucharistic liturgy, the worshipers join with "angels and archangels, and with all the company of heaven" around the throne of God to sing His praises. They celebrate that the work of the Lamb has made them members of the eternal, heavenly community. They share table with the Lamb on earth, just as one day they will share table with Him eternally in heaven; see 19:9. They look forward to the time when their eyes will behold the glory of the heavenly Jerusalem and when the final, nuptial embrace between the Lamb and His Church will become a glorious, eternal reality.

**60A** Revelation addresses a situation in which early Christians were facing the threat of persecution by Rome. The author, living in a penal colony on the island of Patmos, sees Rome as the embodiment of emperor worship—which to accept is to deny the incarnation of God in Jesus. He exhorts his readers not to fight against Rome; God will soon bring about its fall.

**60B** In early days of the empire, many worshiped the spirit of Rome to acknowledge that it had brought peace and justice to the world. They saw the spirit of Rome incarnate in the person of the emperor. Once each year, all within the empire were expected to burn a pinch of incense to the emperor and to declare, "Caesar is Lord!"

**60C** Although Nero (A.D. 54–68) persecuted Christians, his persecution was limited to the vicinity of Rome. Persecution spread more widely during the reign of Domitian, A.D. 81–96.

**60D** Revelation is an apocalyptic writing that resembles Daniel 7–12 in spirit. Some today link the message of Revelation only to the end-times and to the Last Day of history, but this approach is invalid. Those who wish to interpret *some* of the symbols and images in Revelation literally must then (to be consistent) interpret *all* of its symbols and images literally.

**60E** The writer sets out to stun his readers with images and visions. After his introductory chapter, John presents six blocks of materials in which the number seven plays a central role. In chs. 21,22, he describes the New Creation and New Jerusalem that will eventually be established.

**60F** Chs. 2,3 consist of seven letters to seven churches in seven major cities in western Anatolia (present-day Turkey) in the Roman province of Asia. They encourage their readers to remain loyal to Jesus the Messiah in the face of persecution from without and temptation from within.

**60G** Revelation's message spirals. After the seven letters come five sections—each of which spans the period from the writer's day until God intervenes to bring about the Final Day of history. The central message of each section is, "Stand firm! God will deliver you soon!" In presenting his message, the writer makes use of many symbols and numbers—each of which has its own significance.

**60H** The section titled *The Seven Seals* begins with an introductory vision that describes the glory of God and the authority of Jesus in relation to the unfolding of history. Jesus is given a scroll with seven seals. As Jesus removes each seal, its significance in relation to future history is explained.

**60I** In the section titled *The Seven Trumpets*, John describes the desolations that will soon overtake the sinful world in relation to both the created order and the course of history.

**60J** In the section titled *The Seven Signs*, John describes the Roman imperial system as being directed by Satan as it seeks to harass God's people. The Roman priesthood that promoted and supported emperor worship (to its own advantage and profit) will eventually be done away with.

**60K** In the section *The Seven Bowls*, John sees seven angels emptying bowls—an action that brings on a succession of disasters that resemble the plagues in Egypt. Rome is about to be destroyed!

**60L** In the section titled *The Seven Sights*, the judgment and fall of Rome is described. Jesus is declared victorious over the beast (Rome) and the false prophet (the Roman priesthood). Satan is bound—and then released for 1,000 years. God's people are preserved, kept secure, and reign during this final 1,000 years.

**60M** When Jesus finally reappears, so does the eternal dwelling place that God has prepared for His people. The dwelling place has the shape of a cube, with each side measuring 1,500 miles (2,400 kilometers). There is no Temple within it—God's presence fills the entire structure. The "river of life" that flows from it resembles that described in Ezekiel 47:1–12.

**60N** Although Revelation assures God's suffering people that they will finally be rescued from all oppression, it also reminds them that their own lives are under constant scrutiny and there is much in the church that displeases the Risen Lord. Although God's people possess eternal life in *faith*, they enjoy it only in *hope*. They must be prepared to suffer the abuse of this world in patience, persevere in faith in God's grace, practice sincere love for one another—and pray with fervor, "Come, Lord Jesus."